BY PETER K. HOGAN

Edited by Chris Charlesworth
Cover & Book designed by 4i Limited
Picture research by David Brolan

ISBN: 0.7119.3526.2 Order No: OP47334

Exclusive Distributors
Book Sales Limited, 8/9 Frith Street, London W1V 5TZ, UK.
Music Sales Corporation, 257 Park Avenue South, New York, NY 10010, USA.
Music Sales Pty Limited, 30-32 Carrington Street, Sydney, NSW 2000, Australia.

To the Music Trade only:
Music Sales Limited, 8/9, Frith Street, London

All photographs supplied by London Features

Every effort has been made to trace the copyright holders of the pl
two were unreachable. We would be grateful if the photographe

Printed in the United Kingdom by Ebenezer Baylis L

A catalogue record for this book is available from

OMNIBUS PRESS
LONDON · NEW YORK · SYDNEY

Contents

INTRODUCTION v

THE ROYAL FAMILY 1

QUEEN 13
QUEEN II 17
SHEER HEART ATTACK 25
A NIGHT AT THE OPERA 29
A DAY AT THE RACES 37
NEWS OF THE WORLD 41
JAZZ 47
LIVE KILLERS 53
THE GAME 55
FLASH GORDON 61
GREATEST HITS 65
HOT SPACE 71
THE WORKS 77
A KIND OF MAGIC 89
LIVE MAGIC 99
THE MIRACLE 105
INNUENDO 115
GREATEST HITS II 121

DISCOGRAPHY 129

Introduction

Freddie Mercury once succinctly summed up what he felt was the core of Queen's appeal: "I like people to go away from a Queen show feeling fully entertained, having had a good time. I think Queen songs are pure escapism, like going to see a good film – after that, they can go away and say, 'that was great', and go back to their problems.

"I don't want to change the world with our music. There are no hidden messages in our songs, except for some of Brian's. I like to write songs for fun, for modern consumption. People can discard them like a used tissue afterwards. You listen to it, like it, discard it, then on to the next. Disposable pop, yes!"

Disposable pop was what Queen did best, and they did it very well indeed. That's a matter of opinion (mine), and I'm sure there are those who'd argue otherwise – I know people who think Queen's first two albums were their finest hour, but these people are heavy metal fans, so screw them. If I had to define Queen in four words, I'd say: great singles, duff albums. That's an over-simplification, but not by much.

But it's still a major achievement. One shouldn't denigrate the role of disposable pop, and whatever Freddie may have thought, Queen did change the world – if only by brightening up people's lives for three minutes at a time (or, in the case of 'Bohemian Rhapsody', for six minutes), and that's no mean feat. What's more, they managed to do it consistently over a period of decades, and that takes quite a bit of talent. One of the major turning points in Queen's fortunes undoubtedly came with their appearance at Live Aid, when they delivered a 20-minute set that was jam-packed with their hit singles, and millions of viewers were suddenly reminded just how

good this group really was. Queen's 'Greatest Hits' subsequently became the fourth biggest selling album of all time.

It helped that they had one of the most flamboyant frontmen in rock (so much so that the others faded into the background whether they wanted to or not). Freddie Mercury was a consummate showman, a purveyor of flash camp so outrageous that all you could do was laugh. Which was, of course, what he intended, and Mercury's sense of humour may well have been a bigger asset than his voice. Freddie didn't name his band Queen for nothing, but if his glam regalia often looked completely ridiculous, he was usually the first to acknowledge it; and he was also obviously laughing at himself all the way to the bank. "I like to ridicule myself. I don't take myself too seriously," he once said. "I wouldn't wear these clothes if I was serious. The one thing that keeps me going is that I like to laugh at myself."

And that's genuinely endearing. It's a quality we look for in our friends (and in ourselves, if we've got any sense), and it was undoubtedly a large factor in Queen's success. But if Freddie was larger than life, so too were his ambitions: he wanted Queen to be the biggest group ever, and constantly pushed for them to break new territories, and face new challenges. And that drive also had its darker side, as he once admitted: "Excess is part of my nature. Dullness is a disease. I really need danger and excitement."

Freddie Mercury died of AIDS-related bronchial pneumonia. But we have no way of knowing whether the "excess" of his lifestyle was a cause; we do not know how early on Freddie became HIV positive, or whether he contracted the virus through sexual or non-sexual means. It doesn't matter – he's still dead, and AIDS is not a pleasant way to die. It's slow, and it's painful, and anybody who has seen even a glimpse of the disease in action soon stops being judgemental about other people's sexuality. After he died, some of the more homophobic British tabloid newspapers tried to start dredging up a scandal angle... and quickly realised they'd misjudged the sentiments of the British public, who didn't give a toss whether Freddie was gay or not. They'd pretty much assumed he was for years, and didn't care. He made good records, and he was funny, and that was enough.

Not since John Lennon was assassinated has a rock death affected so many, so deeply. And the feelings of Queen's fans echoed those of Lennon's, and it was almost a generational thing – there had been other celebrity AIDS deaths, but with Freddie's passing it felt (for the first time) like we'd lost one of us. As a result, Mercury's death may have made a lot of people re-examine how they viewed other AIDS-sufferers. If so, Freddie would doubtless be pleased, and would perhaps feel that his death had achieved something worthwhile.

His life certainly had. He made good records, and he was funny, and that was more than enough: it was kind of magic.

Peter K Hogan, London 1993

The Royal Family

Queen's début album was recorded at London's Trident Studios between the summer of 1972 and January 1973. By the time it was released, in July 1973, the group had already been together for nearly three years. And Queen were...

Brian May (born on July 19, 1947, in Twickenham, London) had left school with ten 'O'-levels and three 'A'-levels to study astronomy at London's Imperial College – but despite his strong academic background, May's first love was music. He'd been playing guitar from the age of seven, and by fifteen was playing in local bands, jamming with anybody who'd let him. "None of these groups really got anywhere because we never played any real gigs or took it that seriously," he'd recall years later.

There's no truth to the popular rumour that May played on a single by local group The Others ('Oh Yeah', released on Fontana in 1964); he was busily involved at the time with another long-term musical project – building an electric guitar of his own design. Since he couldn't afford the Fender Stratocaster of his dreams, Brian set out – with the help of his father – to create his own personalised guitar. Both father and son were experienced in wood and metal work, and Brian was a star physics student, so the task wasn't quite as difficult as it might sound... though the choice of raw materials was odd, to say the least. (The neck of the guitar is solid mahogany, carved from the surround of a 200-year-old fireplace, the body is solid oak, and the springs of the tremolo unit were salvaged from an old motorbike!) This 'fireplace' guitar has been played on all Queen's hit records, and May still favours it on stage and in the studio to this day. The cost of materials was a mere £8.00. (In 1985, Guild launched a line of authorised copies, which cost considerably more.)

Having decided that a part-time musical involvement wouldn't play havoc with his academic career, Brian continued to gig with '1984', the band he'd formed in late 1964 after arriving at Imperial College in 1965. The high spot of their career came when they supported Jimi Hendrix in September 1967, but they broke up early in 1968 – musical differences and Brian's academic workload being the main reasons. But both Brian and ex-1984 vocalist/bassist Tim Staffell (by then a student at Ealing College of Art) missed being in a band, and decided to form a new one. They placed a note on the Imperial College notice board seeking a "Mitch Mitchell/Ginger Baker type drummer". Quite a few drummers replied and were auditioned, among them a dental student, Roger Taylor. "We thought he was the best drummer we'd ever seen," May later recalled. "I watched him tuning a snare – something I'd never seen done before – and I remember thinking how professional he looked."

Roger Taylor (born Roger Meddows-Taylor on July 26, 1949 in Norfolk) had wanted to be a musician from an early age, and despite some parental disapproval had played in various local groups throughout his teenage years – first as a guitarist, before settling down on a drummer's stool (with a vocal mike as well). After leaving school (with seven 'O'-levels and three 'A'-levels), Taylor came to London in October 1967 to study dentistry at the London Hospital Medical School. His last band, Reaction, broke up in the summer of 1968, leaving Taylor free (and eager) to join forces with May and Staffell .

They christened themselves Smile, and rehearsed through that autumn, playing their first gig at Imperial as support to Pink Floyd. They began gigging regularly on the London pub and college circuit, building a steady following (the hardcore of whom were undoubtedly fellow students from Imperial). Taylor had by this time decided that dentistry probably wasn't for him, and took a year off to concentrate on music. May had already acquired an honours degree in Physics (in 1968), but had remained at Imperial for postgraduate research in Infra-Red Astronomy.

Despite their continuing studies, the three members of Smile were serious about a long-term musical career, but their lack of experience with the music biz led them to sign a less than favourable deal with (ironically enough) Mercury in May 1969. Mercury was an American based label with no real organisation in the UK, other than a distribution deal with Phonogram. They signed Smile to a one-off deal, and sent them into the studio with producer John Anthony. The result was one single, 'Earth' (a Tim Staffell song) backed with 'Step On Me' (a Staffell-May collaboration). The single did absolutely nothing, largely because it was released only in the US (in August 1969), with no group or record company support. Inevitably, it bombed – and because of this was never released in the UK. Mercury gently dropped Smile from their roster.

Disheartened, Tim Staffell quit Smile in the spring of 1970 to form his own group, Humpy Bong, leaving May and Taylor feeling more than a little depressed that summer. In the autumn, May – uncertain whether to continue his research studies – took a job teaching mathematics in a London comprehensive school. In the meantime, Staffell's flatmate joined Roger Taylor in running a second-hand clothes stall in Kensington Market. He was an ex-Art student with very definite ideas about how to run a pop group, and his name was Freddie.

Freddie Mercury was born Frederick Bulsara, on September 5, 1946, on the small island of Zanzibar (which is now part of Tanzania). Both Freddie's parents were of Persian descent, and of the Zoroastrian faith. The young Freddie lived in Zanzibar until age ten, when he began attending boarding school in Bombay, where he remained until sixteen. A revolution in Zanzibar in 1964 forced the Bulsaras to flee to safety in Britain, and Freddie took a number of lowly jobs while studying Art 'A'-level at Isleworth Polytechnic, preparatory to going to art school. In September 1966 he entered Ealing College Of Art (other ex-students include Pete Townshend of The Who, Rolling Stone Ronnie Wood and Roger Ruskin Spear of The Bonzo Dog Doo Dah Band), graduating with a Diploma in Art & Design (equivalent to a degree) three years later. "Art college teaches you to be more fashion conscious, to be always one step ahead," he later said.

In common with many art students of the period, Freddie was intrigued by the possibilities of pop music, and was a keen supporter of his friend Tim's group Smile. He'd had one teenage band at school, and now joined another – a group from Liverpool called Ibex, who needed a vocalist (Freddie also played guitar – though it wasn't his strongest point).

In the summer of 1969, Freddie suggested to Taylor that they share a stall at Kensington Market and, money being scarce, Taylor agreed. They tried selling artwork (their own and that of other students) with little success, but selling second-hand Victorian clothes proved luckier . By this point, Freddie was sharing a house in Barnes with all the members of Smile (and several other people as well). The majority of gigs Ibex managed to get were all in the north of England, and the group thought it more sensible to move back to Liverpool. Freddie reluctantly moved with them, but found the experience grim, returning to London a month later.

Two more bands – Sour Milk Sea and Wreckage – came and went in the next six months, producing little income or success (though doubtless useful for Freddie to hone his stage persona). Nor was there much income otherwise – just a trickle of design work. In a letter to a friend dated October 1969 (which came up for auction at Sotheby's in July 1993), Freddie wrote: "I'm working at Harrods and it's only to pay the rent... Roger and I go poncing and ultrablagging just about everywhere and lately were being termed as a couple of queens." Though Freddie had almost certainly had homosexual experiences while at boarding school, he was by no means exclusively gay at this point, and in the same letter he objects to the fact that a friend has been labelling him "a fully-fledged queer".

In April 1970, Freddie finally joined musical forces with May and Taylor. It seemed inevitable. Both of them were taken with Freddie's ideas, and the fact that he was equally obsessed with Jimi Hendrix and the Hollywood glamour of Dietrich, Garbo and Busby Berkeley. Mercury's plan was simple enough: combine the 'heaviness' of Led Zeppelin with a new kind of visual flair. Outrageousness plus pop sensibility equals success, Freddie argued. Why not ?

At this time, David Bowie was still a folk singer with one fluke pop hit, and glam and glitter had yet to be invented (though Freddie was just the man to do it). His obvious role model was Mick Jagger, who'd been camping it all the way to the bank for years. Let's call the group Queen, suggested Freddie. Why not ?

"Years ago I thought up the name Queen," Mercury later explained. "It's just a name, but it's very regal obviously, and it sounds splendid... It's a strong name, very universal and immediate. It had a lot of visual potential and was open to all sorts of interpretations. I was certainly aware of the gay connotations, but that was just one facet of it." May had wanted to call the group Grand Dance, Taylor's choice being The Rich Kids. Freddie got his way. At the same time, he re-christened himself Mercury after the mythological messenger of the gods, possibly feeling he had a message for someone.

Freddie had been making suggestions right from the start, from the first time he'd seen Smile play live. "Why are you wasting your time doing this?" he'd nag them. "You should do more original material. You should be more demonstrative in the way you put the music across. If I was your singer, that's what I'd be doing." And now he *was* their singer.

But May and Taylor had been soured by their Smile experiences. May had painstakingly built a guitar that was as good if not better than anything commercially available. Freddie had *very* definite ideas about presentation. All of them were intelligent and qualified individuals who could easily have found well-paid jobs in the 'real world', and if they were to form a rock group, they intended to take it seriously, and make a real success of it. Consequently, they took things very slowly. Throughout 1970 they rehearsed and wrote material (all three were songwriters), honing it in live performance at gigs and friends' parties. They had no intention of rushing into anything. After wearing out three bass players in rapid succession, they got lucky, and in February 1971 Queen acquired their final member.

John Deacon (born in Leicester on August 19, 1951) had played in various local teenage groups before moving to London where he studied Electronics (obtaining a first class honours degree six months after joining Queen). Despite being a few years younger, Deacon meshed with the others from the word go. "We just knew he was the right one, even though he was so quiet. He hardly spoke to us at all," Brian would later recall.

"I was possibly the one person in the group who could look at it from the outside, because I came in as the fourth person in the band," said John. "I knew there was something there but I wasn't convinced of it... until possibly the 'Sheer Heart Attack' album."

Now that they had their fourth member, Freddie designed a logo for the group, based on their astrological signs (shades of Spinal Tap but, to be fair, this *was* 1971), and the group were ready to roll. In July 1971 they played their first 'proper' gig, and for most of that summer Queen played various dates around the West Country (using Taylor's contacts), and at Imperial College that autumn. May and Deacon studied; Taylor and Mercury ran their clothes stall. Most of their discussions revolved around turning professional.

Freddie: "We said, 'okay, we're going to take the plunge into rock, and we're really going to do a job at it, no half measures.' We all had potentially good careers and we weren't prepared to settle for second best if we were going to abandon all the qualifications we had got in other fields."

Roger: "For the first two years nothing really happened. We were all studying, but progress in the band was nil. We had great ideas, though, and somehow I think we all felt we'd get through."

Brian: "We all had quite a bit to lose, really, and it didn't come easy. To be honest, I don't think any of us realised it would take a full three years to get anywhere. It was certainly no fairy tale."

Financially, things were still bad. Roger even enrolled to study biology at North London Polytechnic – largely so he could get a grant. He'd given up on Kensington Market, though Freddie stayed on there with a new partner (there are stories of him rigging mirrors so as to spy on the women's changing rooms).

Then, around September 1971, Queen got a real break. The newly-opened De Lane Lea recording studios (in Wembley, North London), were anxious to test out their equipment, and produce some kind of showcase material with which to interest new clients who would be exponents of the then-burgeoning 'heavy rock'. In short, they were actively looking for a group who would be ready to give studio demonstrations to potential clients.

Through Terry Yeadon, a friend of Brian May's working at the studio, Queen got the gig. In return for their services, the group were given unlimited free studio time and could keep all the tapes they recorded. They spent most of the rest of the year making demos (engineered by De Lane Lea's Louie Astin), using all the technology at their disposal to the full, and forging many new contacts. But none of the record companies they approached with demos was interested enough to offer them a deal (including EMI, despite the fact that one of the demos, 'The Night Comes Down', actually ended up on the first Queen album).

Despite the lack of instant success, they remained optimistic. "There was never a doubt, darling, never," Freddie later maintained. "I just *knew* we would make it, and I told everyone who asked just that."

Nor was all this activity the only change in Freddie's life. He'd acquired a steady girlfriend – Mary Austin, manageress of the Kensington High Street boutique Biba. "It took Freddie nearly six months to ask me out," she said later. "I thought he fancied my best friend, so I used to avoid him. One night we were at one of his gigs, and after it had finished he came looking for me. I left him at the bar with my friend to go to the loo, but actually I sneaked out. He was furious !" When the couple finally did get their relationship on course, they were inseparable.

Among the many studio technicians who came to view Queen's set-up at De Lane Lea were former Smile-producer John Anthony, and his colleague Roy Thomas Baker, both staff engineers from Trident Studios off Wardour Street. Baker had also just notched up his first album as fully-fledged producer (the second Nazareth album). When they entered the studio, Queen were running through a new song, 'Keep Yourself Alive'. "I thought it was fabulous," Baker later recalled. "I totally forgot about looking at the studio!"

Both Baker and Anthony were convinced that Queen were just the band they were looking for, and urged Trident's owners, brothers Barry and Norman Sheffield (who were planning to start a record label in addition to their film and studio interests) to sign the group to their new company, Trident Audio Productions. Despite being impressed with the demo tapes they heard, the Trident executives wanted to see Queen perform live, to see if they were as good in the flesh, so in March 1972 Barry Sheffield trooped down to Forest Hill to see them play at a hospital dance. He liked what he saw, and within two months the group was on the verge of signing to Trident, but insisted on there being three separate contracts for production, publishing and management. The band was asking for a lot, but they'd already turned down a record deal from Chrysalis (too small an advance), and perhaps felt that they might as well ask for the best deal possible. Trident agreed to finance and produce the recording of a Queen album, and then place the finished product with a record company. Anthony and Baker would produce, in association with the group themselves. The triple-contracts were drawn

up, though not yet signed, and as a show of good faith Trident bought the group a new PA and new instruments (except for Brian, who was perfectly happy with his own guitar). Though Queen would part company from Trident acrimoniously in 1975, this was potentially too good a deal to turn down at the time.

Not that Trident seemed overly confident about the project. Queen were allowed to use their 24-track studio, but restricted to using 'dead' studio time (when the studio was empty of paying clients), and that meant working some pretty strange hours, even by rock standards: often the group would work from 10 a.m. to 1 p.m., then return to resume work at 4 a.m. the following morning. "It was horrible," Baker later recalled, "but that's how the whole album came together."

Despite these limitations, the group was pleased with the finished record. All that remained to be done was to find a record company to release it. This task fell to Jack Nelson, an American A&R man brought in by Trident to find a deal for Queen and their other signings, a singer called Eugene Wallace, and a group called Mark Ashton and Headstone. Though Nelson found interest in Queen from EMI, Trident wanted an 'all or nothing' deal for all their artists, and EMI turned this down.

Meanwhile, John Deacon finished his degree course in June 1972, and Roger obtained a degree in Biology a couple of months later. In September 1972, though Queen had yet to sign officially with Trident, they were finally put on the payroll, and received £20 each per week – barely enough to cover living costs. They finally signed the Trident contract two months later.

Jack Nelson (who, because of the lack of anyone else likely being around, was effectively the group's manager by now) had still to find a home for the album. "It took me over a year to get Queen a deal, and everyone turned them down, I mean everyone," he said. Nelson was negotiating seriously with CBS when a telegram arrived from Roy Featherstone, who had just heard the Queen tape at the MIDEM festival, and wanted to make them an offer.

It took EMI three months to complete negotiations with Trident (and, in the end, EMI had to accept the other Trident acts as well after all – and whatever happened to *them*?), but Queen officially signed to the label in March 1973.

On April 9, 1973, they played a showcase gig at the Marquee to celebrate their signing to EMI (and give Elektra boss Jac Holzman a chance to see them play live). But the album still wasn't scheduled for release, and didn't reach the shops for another three months. Though the gig got plenty of music press attention, the impetus of a press campaign was lost.

They were still experimenting with their image, and were presently going through a black-and-white phase. Brian May remembers encountering fans in Liverpool who'd adopted the theme to the extent of painting their fingers alternately black and white: "One night after a show they produced their nail varnish bottle and, amidst much drinking, painted Freddie's nails black and mine white. It added to the general effect, so we decided to keep it up. I could only wear white varnish on the left hand, though, because playing scratched it all off the right hand. But in the white and violet lights that we used as footlights they glowed strangely. The nails survived the first couple of tours, as did the eye make-up."

But Freddie was fussy about his appearance. *Incredibly* fussy. Old friend Helen McConnell recalls arriving to pick up Freddie for a night's socialising (he was by now sharing a flat with Mary), only to find him preening himself : "Freddie spent a whole hour in front of the mirror in the bedroom, just choosing which belt to wear! He would come out in each one and ask our opinion. We just wanted to go out! He was so vain, but we tolerated it – everyone did. It was part of him, part of his character. He just wouldn't have been Freddie without that vanity."

As work on the album neared completion, Freddie, Brian and Roger (plus several uncredited others) recorded cover versions of 'I Can Hear Music' (written by Phil Spector and Ellie Greenwich, and a hit for The Beach Boys) and 'Goin' Back' (written by Goffin and King, first recorded by The Byrds). Robin Cable produced the session, and the two songs were released by EMI as a single in June, under the pseudonym 'Larry Lurex' (a spoof of – or possibly a tribute to – Gary Glitter). But Glitter was immensely popular, and possibly because of that this 'pastiche' sank without trace.

Queen

EMI EMC 3006

Queen's first official single, 'Keep Yourself Alive', was finally released on July 6, 1973, to mixed reviews: "If these guys look half as good as they sound, they could be huge" – *NME*; "A raucous, well built single" – *Record Mirror*; "It never really gets going" – *Sounds*; "Lacks originality" – *Melody Maker*.

It was followed by the album, called simply 'Queen' (rejected titles included 'Top Fax, Pix And Info' and 'Deary Me') which was released a week later, on July 13, 1973. Possibly to make up for lost time, EMI launched both single and album with a huge promotional blitz, causing accusations of 'hype' to be hurled within the music press. At the time (in those pre-Malcolm McLaren days), this was a serious insult, and perhaps this is the reason the single was rejected no less than five times by the BBC Radio One playlist. As a result, it received virtually no airplay (the first licensed commercial radio stations didn't come into operation until later that year). Consequently, the single never reached the charts (possibly this is the reason why the song was strangely not included on the 'Queen's Greatest Hits' compilation).

But at least the records were out at last. The sleeve notes boasted that the album represented "at last something of what Queen music has been over the last three years", and you can almost hear the relief that they'd finally completed something on vinyl. They also proudly announced that they didn't use any synthesizers (which many listeners had automatically assumed was what they were hearing; in fact, it was Brian May's distinctive guitar-sound).

The album shows them flirting with glam, and also displays the group's virtuosity: apart from May's guitar, there are Taylor and Deacon's thundering rhythms, some impossibly high harmonies from Freddie, a bit of jazz,

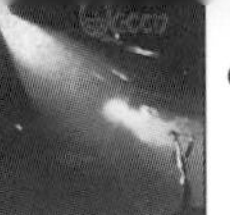

some gentle folk-rock and a *lot* of metal. The result was aimed squarely at the 'heavier' end of the market and – apart from the single (and a short snatch of 'Seven Seas Of Rhye', which would turn up in full on the group's second album the following year) – there's little trace of the pop sensibilities they'd exploit to such success in later years. Today, it sounds both dated and self-indulgent – but then, the same is true of most 'progressive' rock of that era. Still, few critics would go as far as *NME*'s Nick Kent, who dismissed the record as "a bucket of urine" (thus beginning a long-term feud between the group and the rock weekly).

Regardless, Queen had begun to capture public attention. The album spent seventeen weeks on the charts (highest position – No. 24), and qualified for a gold disc. (Two rare versions of the album exist: some advance copies – with unfinished sleeves – were previewed at an EMI sales conference, and there is also a quadraphonic version, which was released in the US only.)

Queen II

EMI EMA 767

Queen had finally left the wilderness, and were on their way and optimistic. In August 1973, just weeks after their first album hit the shops, they returned to the studio to record the follow-up.

In August 1973, Queen began rehearsing new material preparatory to recording. Trident, their management company, booked rehearsal space for the group at Shepperton film studios, on one of the huge sound stages. While there they made promotional films (at the time an almost revolutionary concept) for two songs from the first album, 'Liar' and 'Keep Yourself Alive', with director Mike Mansfield. The finished product was less than inspiring, and – unhappy with both their own performance (their first experience of such work) and with Mansfield's approach – the group insisted that the films be junked. Replacement footage was shot that same month, this time directed by Barry Sheffield and Queen themselves.

Once again, they used Trident Studios and once again Roy Thomas Baker produced – or rather, co-produced with Queen. Their first album had been a mini-history of the material the group had written in their first three years. The second album set out to show what they were capable of *now*. This time around there was no question of having to use 'dead' studio time – Trident booked them in as a major act, and all the studio's resources (including time) were at their disposal. They made full use of the chance to experiment.

Recording was completed within a matter of weeks, and in September Brian May began a part-time job teaching English at Stockwell Manor comprehensive school in South London. He was still considering teaching as a career if the group failed, still working on his thesis and on a computer programme to calcu-

late the positions of guitar frets. If that wasn't enough to keep him out of trouble, he was also working part-time for EMI Electronics, helping to assess the destructive capability of fragmentation bombs. Roger Taylor, meanwhile, contributed percussion to Al Stewart's 'Past, Present And Future' album, which was being recorded at Trident.

Also in September, the group played a one-off concert at the Golders Green Hippodrome, which was recorded by BBC Radio One for their 'In Concert' series and featured material from the new album. Meanwhile, the first album was released in the US by Elektra, gaining some radio interest and reaching No 83 on the *Billboard* chart.

The following month saw them undertaking promotional TV and radio appearances in Belgium, France and Holland, plus one concert in Frankfurt, Germany. The day after the Frankfurt gig they played Le Blow Up in Luxembourg, which was due to be recorded for broadcast by Radio Luxembourg. Unfortunately, equipment failure prevented that from happening.

Finally, at the beginning of November Queen kicked off their first proper nationwide tour, as support to Mott The Hoople, who were at the time a very hot group indeed (thanks largely to the efforts of their writer/producer, David Bowie – who by this time had already made the transition from Beckenham hippie to something else altogether). They played 26 dates before the end of the year (including six solo gigs without Mott), and gathered the beginnings of a strong fan following, as well as a few enthusiastic press mentions. The tour climaxed at Hammersmith Odeon on December 14, where Queen played to their largest audience to date. Mott was so pleased with their support act that they promptly asked them to play support once again for their American tour the following year, and Queen just as promptly agreed. They closed the year with a gig in Liverpool on December 28, supporting 10cc. Further down the bill, the third group – Great Day – included some of Freddie's old mates from his pre-Queen outfit Ibex.

In January 1974 there was good news and bad news. The good news was music paper *Sounds* calling Queen "Britain's biggest unknowns"; the bad news was the fear that Brian May might lose an arm from gangrene.

Queen II

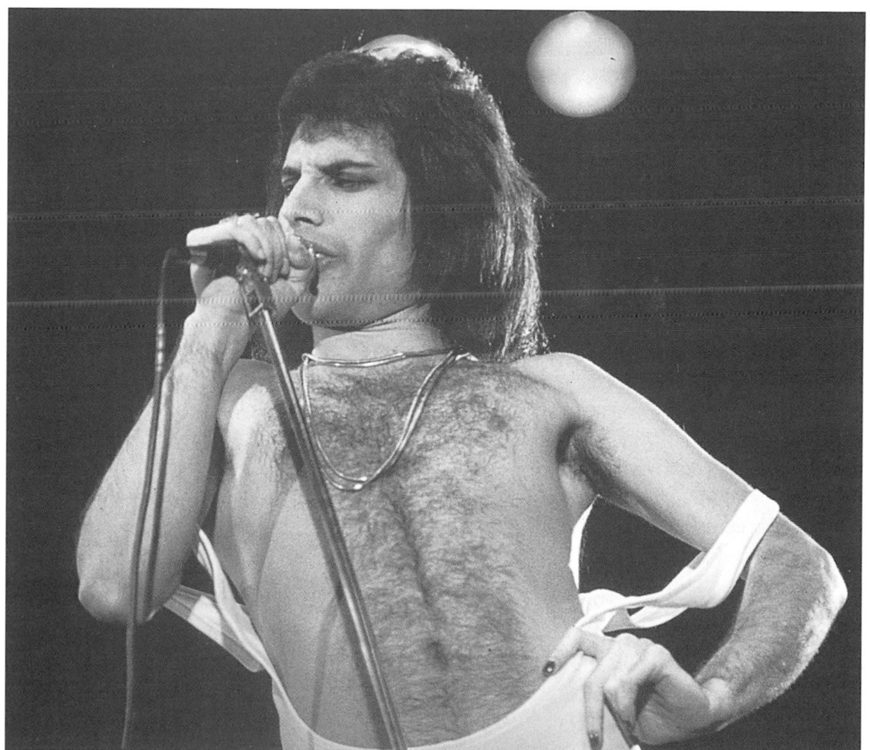

Queen were booked to play two gigs at an Australian music festival at the end of the month, and while receiving the necessary travel inoculations Brian contracted an infection from a dirty needle, resulting in a high fever and a hugely swollen arm. Fortunately, the infection subsided.

But Australia was a nightmare. The Australians couldn't figure out what an unknown British group was doing there, and suspected hype. The fact that they arrived at the festival site in white limousines marked them down as 'stuck-up pommies', and they were even introduced as such to the crowd. Not only that, but the sound system was terrible, their lighting rig was sabotaged and Brian's arm was still causing him a lot of pain, making it difficult for him to play. Worse, Freddie was on antibiotics for an ear infection, and the pills affected his hearing. Not the grooviest of gigs. The following day they cancelled the second gig due to Freddie's illness and flew home. To add insult to injury, they had to pay their own return air fares... and arriving jet lagged and exhausted were surprised at Heathrow by a battery of photographers who'd been told to expect Her Majesty Queen Elizabeth II instead!

Things could only get better, and they did. In February EMI promo man Ronnie Fowler – who'd been relentlessly playing a white label of the first single from the forthcoming new Queen album to anyone who'd listen – managed to get the group a last-minute slot on *Top Of The Pops*. In those days groups rarely performed live on the show, but although the BBC didn't mind miming they refused to allow groups to mime to their actual records; instead, groups had to re-record a special backing track. Fowler had to book the group into a studio that night on only a few hours notice (The Who's Pete Townshend obliged by giving up some of his booked studio time); with their newly completed backing track, Queen turned up at the BBC the next day to record their first TV appearance, promoting a single – 'Seven Seas Of Rhye' – that wasn't even released yet !

EMI rush-released the single, and it was in the shops on February 23, two days after the TV show aired. In the intervening time, Fowler had saturated Radio One with white labels of the single... but on hearing the song played on the radio, Freddie Mercury insisted they be

withdrawn, as they'd been given the wrong mix of the song. Fowler managed to swap all but two copies of the white label for ones with the correct mix (those missing two must be among the rarest Queen records of all !) The single was obviously destined to be a hit, and even got a good review from the *NME*: "This single showcases all their power and drive, their writing talents, and every quality that makes them unique." Smelling success on the breeze, Freddie finally gave up working on his stall in Kensington Market.

The album was ready for release, but was postponed when the group spotted a serious error on the record sleeve's credits – and John Deacon didn't much care for his accidental rechristening as Deacon John. Release was further delayed by the British government who – because of a serious oil crisis – had imposed a three-day working week on the people of Britain. Severe restrictions on the use of electricity crippled EMI's pressing plant, and it soon became obvious that the album would not be in the shops in time for the start of Queen's first headlining tour of the UK.

Undismayed, the group began rehearsals (at Ealing film studios) for the tour. Designer Zandra Rhodes was commissioned to design their stage costumes (based on Freddie's ideas). On March 1, the tour kicked off in Blackpool, and though there were a few minor problems (a gig in Aylesbury was cut short by Brian's still-painful arm trouble – and Freddie brought one soundcheck to a complete halt when his silver bracelet flew off stage, refusing to continue until he'd recovered it) the tour was an enormous success right from the start. One night the audience started singing 'God Save The Queen' while waiting for the group to come on stage – something that became a fixture at their gigs from then on.

On March 5, 'Seven Seas Of Rhye' entered the charts at 45, and three days later Queen II was finally released. EMI pulled out all the promotional stops (possibly because they were annoyed that Queen's US label Elektra had achieved greater success with the group's début album than they had), but reviews were mixed. "This album captures them in their finest hours," said *Sounds*, while the *Melody Maker* reviewer observed, "It's currently in the balance whether they'll really break through here. If they do, then I'll have to eat my hat or something. Maybe Queen try too

hard – there's no depth of sound or feeling." *Record Mirror* were even more scathing: "This is it, the dregs of glam rock. Weak and over-produced, if this band are our brightest hope for the future, then we are committing rock and roll suicide."

On the plus side, Queen II was slicker (and a lot gentler) than its predecessor; on the minus, the group was still prone to self-indulgence in a big way. With its references to White and Black Queens, Fairies and Ogres, the record comes perilously close to being that dreaded animal of the Seventies: the concept album. The media had quickly sussed Freddie's ambivalent sexuality (practically *de rigueur* in the early Seventies), and he played it for all it was worth. "I just like people to put their own interpretation on my songs. Really, they are just little fairy stories," Mercury told *NME*, his tongue firmly in his cheek. Asked more directly about the subject, he admitted, "I'm as gay as a daffodil, dear", while Taylor conceded: "Freddie's just his natural self; just a poof, really."

But, as with the first album, much of the second album has not stood the test of time at all well – though (again) the same could be said of most 'progressive' rock of that era. There's only one truly memorable tune included (in fact, it's the only track that displays any pop sensibility, or even sounds at all like the group Queen fans would later come to know and love), and that's 'Seven Seas of Rhye' (which had had a mini-preview as the closing instrumental of the first album). The single hit the charts everywhere from Tooting through Tulsa to Tokyo. In Britain, it reached Number 10.

As for the album, it reached number five on the British album charts, staying there for over seven months. Not only that, but interest in the group's début outing was rekindled, and that also re-entered the charts (at number 24). Meanwhile Queen continued their tour, in the course of which John Deacon decided to abandon his MSc studies in order to commit his energies fully to the group.

At Stirling University in Scotland the crowd was so enthusiastic that the group played three encores... but when they (quite reasonably) refused to return to the stage for a fourth, fights broke out in the crowd and the police were called in. Two fans were stabbed, and two members of the road crew

were hospitalised. The following night's concert in Birmingham was postponed till the end of the tour, after a triumphant London gig at the Rainbow.

During the tour the group granted another interview to *NME* journalist Julie Webb, in the course of which Freddie complained about some of the criticism the group had been getting in the press: "I think, to an extent, we're a sitting target because we gained popularity quicker than most bands, and we've been talked about more than any other band in the last month, so it's inevitable. Briefly, I'd be the first one to respect fair criticism. I think it would be wrong if all we got were good reviews... but it's when you get unfair, dishonest reviews where people haven't done their homework that I get annoyed." Asked about his days at boarding school, Freddie replied: "All the things they say about them are more or less true. All the bullying and everything else. I've had the odd schoolmaster chasing me. It didn't shock me because somehow boarding schools... you're not confronted by it, you are just slowly aware of it." After Freddie admitted that he'd been "considered the arch poof" at school, Webb asked him outright whether he was gay. "You crafty cow," replied Mercury. "Let's put it this way – there were times when I was young and green. It's a thing schoolboys go through. I've had my share of schoolboy pranks. I'm not going to elaborate further."

On April 12 Queen flew to the United States to begin their first American tour, again as Mott The Hoople's support act. The tour was strenuous, but the audiences were (largely) receptive and the band thoroughly enjoyed themselves. Then, on May 12, during the last of six nights the Mott/Queen package had played at the Uris Theater on Broadway in New York, Brian May collapsed. A doctor diagnosed hepatitis (the delayed result of May's earlier arm infection), and ordered May to strict bed rest for six weeks. The group had no choice but to cancel the remainder of the tour. Kansas stepped in to replace them as Mott's support, and everyone (bands, road crews, journalists – quite a few people in total) who'd had contact with May had to be inoculated against hepatitis.

So Queen flew home to lick their wounds, and a very disheartened Brian May ("I felt I had let everyone down") took to his sickbed to write new material for the group's third album, 'Sheer Heart Attack'.

QUEEN
SHEER
HEART
ATTACK

Sheer Heart Attack

EMI EMC 3061

In early June 1974, Queen began rehearsing songs for the new album at Rockfield Studios in Wales, writing additional material as they went along. But Brian May was still seriously ill, often disappearing to the bathroom to throw up.

Recording proper began at Trident on July 15, and progressed well until the recording sessions were scuppered when May was rushed into Kings College Hospital suffering from yet another health problem – this time a duodenal ulcer. An emergency operation went fine, but a period of convalescence was needed... which meant that Queen were effectively out of action, and a US tour planned for that September had to be cancelled. May was extremely depressed (by now, he must have felt he was jinxed), and convinced that the group would simply replace him. Which, of course, they didn't even consider; with the aid of Roy Thomas Baker (by now known as the 'fifth Queenie') they managed to plough on with the recording, leaving gaps for Brian's guitar parts to be added later (which is not as easy as it sounds). As May later recalled, "When I finally got out of hospital there was, of course, a mountain of playing to catch up on, plus the vocal harmony parts that needed the depth of the three voices. We did much of the overdubbing in London. We finished off 'Killer Queen', 'She Makes Me' (complete with authentic New York nightmare sounds) and 'Brighton Rock'. 'Now I'm Here' was started and finished in the last couple of weeks, since I'd finally got my ideas straight for the song while in hospital, reflecting on the Mott tour and the future."

And, against all the odds, Queen pulled it off, producing the album that would finally convince John Deacon that he'd joined the right group. In a sense, this was the first 'proper' Queen album – the emphasis was less on

instrumental solos, and more on hummable pop songs, notably 'Killer Queen', Mercury's ode to a high-class call girl ("classy people can be whores too," Mercury explained). The song was released as a single in October 1974, and reached number two (it was kept off the number one slot by teenybopper idol David Essex). The song was also a hit with the critics ("Queen have come up with a sound that'll prove they aren't any one-hit band," said *NME*), although by this point Queen were heartily sick of their press treatment and turned down virtually all requests for interviews (which only made relations with the press even worse).

May later said that 'Killer Queen' was "the turning point. It was the song that best summed up our kind of music, and a big hit, and we desperately needed it as a mark of something successful happening for us. We were penniless, you know, just like any other struggling rock'n' roll band. All sitting around London in bedsitters, just like the rest."

At the end of October, they kicked off a UK tour, and encountered serious Queenmania: in Liverpool and Leeds fans rushed the stage when Queen came on, though fortunately no one got hurt. And at Glasgow Apollo on November 8, Freddie was dragged into the crowd by enthusiastic fans, and had to be rescued by security guards. Ten rows of seats were damaged, but the Apollo's manager was still pleased – it was the first time the venue had sold out. The same day, 'Sheer Heart Attack' appeared in the shops.

Third albums are traditionally regarded as the acid test of a group's talent and potential longevity... and Queen's passed the test with flying colours; if it wasn't *exactly* dynamite with a laser beam, it at least showed that they were capable of generating serious sparks.

"People didn't like it at the time," Roy Thomas Baker said later, "because they thought it was a bit over the top, which it was. It had every conceivable production idea that was available to us." But though relations between the rock press and Queen were still strained (Queen would later claim that the weekly music papers invented most of the Queen 'quotes' they published), the album *did* get favourable notices at the time: "A feast," said *NME*'s reviewer. "No duffers, and four songs that will just run and run: 'Killer Queen', 'Flick Of The Wrist', 'Now I'm Here'

and 'In The Lap Of The Gods... Revisited'. Even the track I don't like, 'Brighton Rock', includes May's Echoplex solo, still a vibrant, thrilling experience whether you hear it live or on record."

The UK tour concluded with two nights at London's Rainbow Theatre, both of which were filmed (for a possible feature film) and recorded (for a possible live album). The live album idea was shelved, as the band felt it wouldn't be a good move at this early date in their career.

'Sheer Heart Attack' marked a serious turning point in Queen's fortunes. Both the album and 'Killer Queen' reached number two on the charts (the latter was the group's first US hit). In the UK, all three Queen albums to date were on the charts at the same time.

Queen

A Night At The Opera

A Night At The Opera

EMI EMTC 103

At the end of November Queen began a European tour, playing Scandinavia, Belgium, Germany and Spain. Everywhere they played their concerts sold out, and the new album was selling well. It even reached the Top Ten in the US, which boded well for their next tour there. They returned to Britain in December, and the group appeared on the Granada TV show 45 on Christmas Day.

Also in December, Queen approached Jim Beach, an up and coming music biz lawyer, with a view to extricating themselves from the three-contract Trident deal. Basically, they'd had enough of being underpaid. With 'Sheer Heart Attack' their wages had risen from £20 each per week to £60, but it was still nowhere near what their success indicated they *should* have been earning. Furthermore, even given the prospect of their future royalties, Trident refused to advance them any cash; John Deacon wanted to buy a small house (he married his long-time girlfriend Veronica Tetzlaff in January 1975) and needed £4,000 for the deposit, but Trident refused to lend it to him. Freddie's request for a new piano and Roger's plea for a small car also fell on deaf ears. So Beach began discussions about freeing the group from their management, but the negotiations would drag on acrimoniously for another nine months.

Queen kicked off their sell-out ('Killer Queen' had reached number five) nation-wide US tour on February 5, 1975, and this time – with massive backing from Elektra – they were headlining (support acts were Kansas, Mahogany Rush and – occasionally – Styx). But critics compared them (unkindly) with Led Zeppelin and, once again, health problems scuppered the tour; this time the victim was Freddie, who developed problems with his voice half-way through. When his voice went

completely in Philadelphia, he saw a throat specialist and was diagnosed as having suspected throat nodules – a common singer's complaint, but still a serious one. The doctor told Freddie to avoid singing (and, as far as possible, speaking) for the next three months. Freddie played one more gig, then flew to New York for a second opinion. This time the verdict was more optimistic – Freddie didn't have nodes after all (a big relief, since this might have necessitated an operation), but simply a badly swollen throat which needed plenty of rest. A third throat specialist in New Orleans confirmed this diagnosis, loaded Freddie down with antibiotics and painkillers, and again ordered a complete rest. The next six concerts were cancelled, but it turned out not to have been enough; when the tour resumed, more concerts had to be cancelled when Freddie's condition recurred.

While on the road in the States, the group met and talked with Don Arden with a view to him becoming their manager once they were free from Trident – to which the band agreed in principle, if Arden was able to come to an arrangement with Trident for their release.

While negotiations proceeded (slowly) in England, the group grabbed a short holiday in Hawaii before starting their first tour of Japan. Both the album and single were at number one when Queen arrived in Tokyo that April for an 11-date tour. And they were treated royally – the biggest thing to hit Japan since The Beatles. Their first Tokyo concert nearly turned into tragedy as the crowd of fans surged dangerously towards the stage, but Freddie managed to calm them down. Even so, Queen had to be escorted from the gig in an armoured car. "It was amazing," May later recalled. "All these little Japanese people screaming and yelling for *us*. We couldn't take it all in – it was like another world, but we loved it!" Freddie especially fell in love with the country, subsequently becoming a collector of Japanese art and curios.

Returning to England, Freddie was presented with an Ivor Novello Award for 'Killer Queen', and the group began rehearsals for their next album – their most ambitious project to date. The plan was to deliberately create a 'classic' album (in all senses of the word), using state-of-the-art technology... but no synthesizers. Queen still believed that real instru-

ments were preferable – and besides, Brian May seemed able to produce just about any desired sound on his guitar.

But despite two months spent rehearsing the material, the album kept on growing. 'A Night At The Opera' was recorded in six different studios over the next five months (often with band members in different studios at the same time !). The drum tracks were recorded at Rockfield, while multi-tracked vocals were recorded at the Roundhouse studios and May's layered guitar parts were recorded at Sarm. Slowly, Roy Thomas Baker laboriously pieced the whole jigsaw together. In August, May and Mercury also contributed guitar, piano and vocals to singer-songwriter Eddie Howell's single 'Man From Manhattan' (released the following month), and in July John and Veronica Deacon became the parents of a son, Robert.

In August Queen were also finally able to sever their connections with Trident (though a planned US tour arranged by Trident had to be cancelled, causing the group quite a bit of financial trouble and adverse publicity, which had them rumoured to be on the verge of a break-up. Brian May was even asked to join Sparks, but declined). Freed from the three Trident contracts, Queen took their music publishing to EMI, then signed their own record deals with EMI and Elektra. But in return for their freedom, they agreed to give Trident a severance payment of £100,000, plus a one per cent royalty on the next six Queen albums. Queen needed to find the money, and they needed a new manager.

In the end, the discussions with Don Arden had come to nothing. Queen were approached by Led Zeppelin's manager Peter Grant, but the two parties were unable to work out a deal. Finally, they settled on Elton John's manager John Reid, and signed with him in September 1975. Reid's first achievement on Queen's behalf was to raise the £100,000 needed to pay off Trident, which he did by getting an advance from EMI against future music publishing royalties. Mercury was ecstatic about leaving Trident: "As far as Queen are concerned, our old management is deceased. They cease to exist in any capacity with us whatsoever. One leaves them behind like so much excreta. We feel so relieved!" But the rift with Trident had left deep scars, as Freddie

Queen
A Night At The Opera

later admitted in a 1977 *Sounds* interview: "It brought on things I never realised. Trust became a very funny word... you just had to keep your defences up."

At least the album had turned out as well as the group had hoped. It would contain what most people now regard as the group's *magnum opus*: the multi-tracked, operatic 'Bohemian Rhapsody'. Alone, this song took over three weeks to record (seven days on the vocals alone), featured 180 vocal overdubs and enough guitar parts to drown out a real orchestra. According to Roy Thomas Baker, "It wasn't all recorded in one go. We did the whole of the first section and the rock section, and for the middle part we just hit some drums now and then – after which it was basically edits. We just lengthened the middle section depending on what vocals were put in, because Freddie would come up with amazing ideas. He'd walk in and say, 'I've got some ideas for the vocals – we'll stick some Galileos in here'...

"The basic backing track was done over a two-day period. The opera section was done over a seven day period of at least ten to twelve hours a day continual singing, and also continual laughing, because it was so funny to do that we were all in hysterics while it was being recorded. Then there were all the guitar overdubs and getting on for two days to mix it. I'd say that that track, on its own, took getting on for three weeks, because it's three songs merged together to make this one track."

Mercury later maintained that the song "didn't just come out of thin air. I did a bit of research, although it was tongue in cheek and it was mock opera. Why not? I certainly wasn't saying I was an opera fanatic and I knew everything about it."

The song was released as a single on Hallowe'en. This was largely due to a helping hand from DJ Kenny Everett. John Reid had been nervous about releasing the song as a single, fearful that its length (six minutes) would result in zero radio airplay, but the group was adamant, refusing to even consider editing the song (Freddie: "We have been forced to make compromises, but cutting up a song will never be one of them!"). The group gave Everett an advance acetate of the song, making him promise not to play it on the air but guessing (and undoubtedly hop-

ing) that he'd go ahead and play it anyway. And he did. Everett played the single fourteen times that weekend; the result was that on Monday morning record shops throughout the land were under siege, and EMI's hand was forced by the sheer number of advance orders for a single which hadn't even been officially announced. Though nobody could ever figure out what the opera was *about*, (the most Freddie would ever say was that it was about personal relationships), the song's sheer uniqueness (in 1975 TV commercials hadn't yet discovered opera) made it an unstoppable hit.

The group previewed the new album to the media at a promotional party at Roundhouse Studios, announcing that it was the most expensive album ever made. But it nearly became a lot *more* expensive when Norman Sheffield of Trident threatened to sue both Queen and EMI for libel, over the song 'Death On Two Legs'. The song was subtitled 'dedicated to...', and Mr Sheffield must have assumed that the dedication was meant for him, as was the sheer vitriol of the lyrics ("you've taken all my money"), despite the fact that Queen had never named names, in print or verbally. EMI eventually settled with Sheffield out of court.

In mid-November, Queen began a nationwide tour... but 'Bohemian Rhapsody' was racing up the charts, and they also wanted to be able to promote the song on TV. The solution was a hastily made (while they were rehearsing) promotional film for the song, directed by *Live At The Rainbow* director Bruce Gowers. It took four hours to make (plus a day to edit), and cost £4,500 – a lot of money in those days, but worth it. The novelty value of a pop mini-film (still a largely unexploited area) gained them plenty of TV airplay – possibly more than they would have got in person!

'A Night At The Opera' (named after the Marx Brothers movie) was released on November 21, and its broad pop approach gained them a whole new audience. The review in *Melody Maker* read: "The overall impression is of musical range, power and consistently incisive lyrics. My hair is still standing on end – so if you like good music and don't mind looking silly, play this album." With its multi-layered guitars and vocals, its

mixture of music hall and pop (territory almost unexplored by anybody except Ray Davies), plus Freddie's flirtations with operatic style, the album was like nothing else around. It's still probably Queen's most cohesive and realised album – a collection of immensely hummable pop songs that stands as the 'Sgt Pepper's' of the post-Glam generation, and worth buying for 'Love Of My Life' alone.

Four days after the album was released, 'Bohemian Rhapsody' went to Number One. The group were understandably delighted, as Roger Taylor's mother later recalled: "We were in a hotel in Southampton – we were there for a gig or something – as the band were all staying in the same place, and I had popped out. When I came back I bumped into John Deacon in the lobby, and he said they were Number One. I was really pleased, and Roger was excited, but it didn't really sink in. Then, on the way home in the car, they played the song on the radio, saying it was Britain's Number One. I suddenly realised that my son was a huge success – he really had made it. It was quite emotional."

The song stayed at Number One for the next nine weeks (breaking a record held since 1957 by Slim Whitman's 'Rosemarie'), selling over a million in the UK alone. It won Freddie another Ivor Novello Award, and would (much later on) provide one of the best scenes in *Wayne's World*, but that's another story...

Queen wound up their UK tour and celebrated their triumph with a televised concert from Hammersmith Odeon for *The Old Grey Whistle Test* on Christmas Eve, which proved that their stage costumes were becoming increasingly flashy and elaborate – a reflection of their new-found confidence and success. Three days after the *Whistle Test*, the album hit the number one slot (it also went platinum, and reached number four in the States).

But they nearly hadn't made it this far, as Mercury later recalled: "At one point, two or three years after we began, we nearly disbanded. We felt it wasn't working, there were too many sharks in the business and it was all getting too much for us. But something inside us kept us going and we learned from our experiences, good and bad... We didn't make any money until the fourth album, 'A Night At The Opera'. Most of our income was consumed by litigation and things like that."

Queen
A Day At The Races

A Day At The Races

EMI EMTC 104

Queen spent the first four months of 1976 touring the States, Japan and Australia. While in New York, the whole group (minus Deacon) visited former Mott singer Ian Hunter in the studio. Hunter was making a solo album ('All American Alien Boy', released that February) with Roy Thomas Baker as producer. As Taylor later recalled, "We spent plenty of time catching up on gossip and tour news, and we all ended up singing backing vocals on one of the tracks, called 'You Nearly Did Me In', which also featured the late great bass player Jaco Pastorius."

In March, Queen's feature film *Queen At The Rainbow* was released, as support to a movie called *The Hustle*; in May the group returned to the UK, and immediately began work on a follow-up to 'Opera'. And for the first time, they were producing themselves, having parted company from Roy Thomas Baker. The split was apparently an amicable one – both parties seemingly just wanted to try something new.

Brian May and his girlfriend Chrissy Mullen got married on May 29, and on June 18 'You're My Best Friend' was released as a single. The *Sounds* review read: "It'll be an absolute smash – beautiful harmonies, strident guitar chords and Freddie in superb voice. Instant number one!" In fact, it reached number seven.

Recording sessions were interrupted for a few gigs in September, two in Edinburgh and one in Cardiff, and – most notably – one as headliners of a free concert in London's Hyde Park on September 18 (the other acts were Kiki Dee, Steve Hillage and Supercharge). Material from the forthcoming album was previewed at all the gigs.

Free concerts had been a regular summer occurrence in Hyde Park since 1968 (the most

publicised being the Stones' 1969 outing). Over 150,000 fans got to see Queen perform, and a splendid time was had by just about everybody (and why can't we have free rock concerts *now*, eh ? If it's okay for Pavarotti, how come it's not okay for Suede? Answer me that...) Brian May has especially fond memories of the day: "The Hyde Park gig was really high. The occasion rather than the gig, you know, the tradition of Hyde Park. I went to the first one, with the Floyd and Jethro Tull – a great atmosphere, and the feeling that it was free. We felt that it would be nice to revive that, but it was fraught with heartache because there were so many problems. Trying to get the place was hard enough, let alone in the evening. We had to make compromises and in the end, because the schedule overran by half an hour, the loss meant we couldn't do an encore."

At the end of the set the crowd was still yelling for more, but Queen – having agreed in advance to a strict time limit for the show – were ordered by the police not to return to the stage. As tour manager Gerry Stickells later recalled, "The police threatened to arrest Freddie if he tried to go back out on stage, as he was furious at having no chance for an encore and was going to go back on and give the crowd what they were yelling for. But the thought of being in jail in tights didn't appeal to him at all, so he gave up!" In the end the police literally pulled the plug, not only cutting off the sound but also plunging the park into total darkness.

The group finished recording 'A Day At The Races' in mid-October, and the first single was released in November to great anticipation (it had been getting advance radio play – thanks largely once again to Kenny Everett – for several weeks). But if 'Somebody To Love' wasn't another 'Bohemian Rhapsody', nobody really expected it to be. It still reached number four.

On December 10, 1976, 'A Day At The Races' was released with advance UK orders of half a million. But if the single was above average, the album was a *big* disappointment. Overconfident in the wake of the success of 'Opera', the group had made the worst mistake possible: they had tried to recreate the 'Opera' formula – even to the extent of nicking another Marx Brothers title. (Groucho Marx had sent a congratulatory telegram to the

group at the album's launch party on Kempton Racecourse; the following year they got to meet him in person in Los Angeles. They sang him one of their songs, and he sang them some of his.) But it just hadn't worked.

Possibly – minus Baker – they were unsure of themselves. They were *definitely* too self-conscious, and the results (Strauss meets Gilbert & Sullivan, basically) are syrupy and sickly; all soft centres and no nuts. The album only really comes to life on two songs: the call and response swingalong sway of 'Somebody To Love', and the kitsch swish of 'Good Old Fashioned Lover Boy'; the rest is not so much filler as goo, and the review in *Sounds* was a fair summation: "It is too formulated, too smartass, too reliant on trickery as a substitute for inspiration. Although I believe that Queen have produced some of the most impressive, majestic, sophisticated music of the decade over the last few years, there has to be a substance behind the frills."

It made little difference to the sales figures, and once again, Queen had a number one album for Christmas.

Also in December, Queen withdrew at the last moment from appearing on Thames TV's *Today* programme. The hastily recruited substitute was a group called The Sex Pistols, who used this unexpected media opportunity to swear their way into the next day's headlines. Punk rock had arrived.

QUEEN

NEWS OF THE WORLD

News Of The World

EMI EMA 748

The very next single to be released by EMI after Queen's 'Somebody To Love' was the Sex Pistols' 'Anarchy In The UK' – and though the Pistols' stay on the label was a brief (but colourful) one, the record set the tone for the year to come. In 1977 punk exploded onto a staid and rather dull music scene – and Queen represented everything that the punks thought had gone wrong with pop. Punk bands rejected the star system utterly, identifying themselves as being on the same level as their audience. You couldn't do that with a band like Queen... not unless you happened to be rich and glamorous, anyway. And the sheer vitality of the punk bands gave credence to their claim that the established acts of the previous decade – including Queen – were decadent, complacent, totally out of touch with their audience, and destined to go the way of the dinosaurs. History has proved them (at least partially) wrong, but at the time there was definitely a generation gap within rock.

But if Queen were the 'older generation', at least they weren't phased by the thought of touring with bands younger (and supposedly wilder) than themselves. They began the year with a three-month tour of North America with Thin Lizzy in support, and Brian May positively relished the prospect of touring with Phil Lynott and Co: "Thin Lizzy as a support band is a real challenge. They'll want to blow us off stage, and that can be a very healthy thing. You feed off the energy of others, and I know that if they go down a real storm then we're gonna go on feeling that much higher. It makes for good concerts. We've had it the other way round. I think we gave Mott The Hoople a hard time on our first tours of Britain and America." Now they were playing larger venues like Madison Square Garden and the LA Forum – they'd finally made it in the States... though the more fashionable critics slammed Queen, and raved about Lizzy.

But the tour still went well, despite a recurrence of Freddie's voice problems (though only two shows had to be cancelled this time).

After the States, the group took a month off to relax in Britain. They all had their own houses now: John and Veronica Deacon in Putney, Brian and Chrissy May in Barnes, Roger and his girlfriend Dominique Beyrand in Fulham. Freddie contented himself with a flat (but it *was* in Kensington), which he shared with Mary. Though their relationship would soon cease to be romantic, they remained the closest of friends until his death. Roger had also bought a country house in Surrey, where he built a home recording studio in the basement; frustrated by the fact that not all the music he wanted to play could be fitted into the Queen format, he was beginning to prepare material for a solo album.

In May they went back on the road – this time to Scandinavia, Europe and the UK – with Freddie demonstrating his love of ballet by wearing a replica of a costume once worn by Nijinsky. On May 20 they released the imaginatively titled 'Queen's First EP', a 4-track sampler ('Good Old-Fashioned Lover Boy', 'Death On Two Legs', 'Tenement Funster' and 'White Queen'). Despite the fact that all the tracks had been available previously, it still made number seventeen in the charts.

At the same time as The Sex Pistols were celebrating Queen Elizabeth II's Silver Jubilee (and topping the charts) with the anti-monarchist 'God Save The Queen', Queen were winding up their British tour with two nights at London's Earl's Court in early June as part of the *official* Jubilee celebrations (proceeds from the second night were donated to the Queen Elizabeth II Jubilee Fund). Queen put on a lavish show (losing £75,000 in the process, so costly were their lighting effects). The Pistols couldn't play *anywhere* at the time, so great was the anti-punk feeling among the general population, and *their* Jubilee gig took place on a boat (which was raided by the River Police). Freddie was unrepentant about siding with the establishment: "The Jubilee's quite fun, isn't it? I love the Queen. I'm very patriotic. I love all this pomp, of course I do. I love it. She does outrageous things!"

In the music press, this didn't exactly go down well. Hawkish young journalists were (obviously) championing the new, young bands, to whom someone like Freddie – who'd often toast his audience with champagne, while decked out in a silver Lurex leotard – seemed

the essence of all that was wrong with rock. The *Sounds* review of 'First EP' read, "Enough to make one paint 'Art Rock Sucks' on a t-shirt", while *NME* ran what was less an interview than a confrontation between Mercury and journalist Tony Stewart under the headline 'Is This Man A Prat?' Communication between the two was almost impossible: to Freddie rock bespoke glamour and always had done. He refused to pretend otherwise, however unfashionable it may have seemed at the time.

Brian May commented on the rock media's attitude towards them: "We were just totally ignored for so long, then completely slagged off and slated by everyone. In a way that was a good start for us. There's no kind of abuse that wasn't thrown at us. It was only around the time of 'Heart Attack' that it began to change.

"I'm always affected by criticism. I think most artists are, even if they say they're not. It doesn't matter how far you get, if someone says you're a load of shit, it hurts."

Mercury was more philosophical: "I just like to think that we've come through rock'n'roll, call it what you like, and there are no barriers: it's open. Especially now, when everybody's putting their feelers out and they want to infiltrate new territories. This is what I've been trying to do for years. Nobody's incorporated ballet. I mean, it sounds *so* outrageous and so extreme, but I *know* there's going to come a time when it's commonplace.

"The term rock'n'roll is just a label one starts off with. I should like to think of it as a vast open door. We just carry on doing as many things as we can in different fields. Labels are confusing, they bounce off me. People want art. They want showbiz. They want to see you rush off in your limousine. If everything you read about me in the press was true, I would have burnt out by now. We will stick to our guns, and *if* we're worth anything, we will live on."

May had also been reported as saying that he and Mercury hardly knew each other, to which Freddie responded in a *Sounds* interview: "It's true, to a certain extent. I want my privacy, and I feel I've given a lot for it."

Queen spent July to September recording the next album at Basing Street and Wessex... while, ironically, the Pistols were recording 'Never Mind The Bollocks' in the studio next door. As Roger Taylor recalls: "One day Sid Vicious stumbled in and yelled at Freddie, 'Ullo, Fred – so you've really brought ballet to the masses, then?' Freddie

just turned round and said, 'Ah, Mr. Ferocious... Well, we're trying our best, dear!'"

May also joined Ringo Starr, Elton John, Ron Wood, Leo Sayer and others to play on Lonnie Donegan's comeback album, 'Puttin' On The Style', contributing guitar to a version of 'Diggin' My Potatoes'. Taylor, meanwhile, released his first solo single – a cover of The Parliaments' a capella doo-wop 'I Wanna Testify'. Taylor's version was no longer a capella, and he played all the instruments himself.

The first fruit of the new Queen album, 'We Are The Champions' (b/w 'We Will Rock You') was released as a single on October 7. *NME* was predictably scathing: "Sounds like it's intended to be adopted by football fans all over the country, making it an instant hit on the terraces. Not a bad idea for a load of balls." The song did indeed become a standard crowd sing-along number at sporting events of every kind. In Britain it reached number two, and in the States (where the two songs were promoted as a double-A side) the single was their biggest success to date, reaching number four and going Platinum.

In October the group won a special Britannia Award (presented by the British Phonographic Industry) for 'Bohemian Rhapsody', which the BPI deemed the "best British single for the past twenty-five years". Gratifying as this must have been for Queen, it also demonstrated that the BPI had (and has) very little grip on reality – had they *really* forgotten The Beatles so quickly? Eleven days later, on October 28, they released the new album, 'News Of The World', produced by themselves with assistance from Mike Stone. The cover art – of a giant robot – was by Frank Kelly Freas, and the original version had been spotted by Taylor on the cover of the pulp science-fiction anthology magazine *Astounding Science*.

'News Of The World' showed the band back on form – rockier, and with not a shred of modesty: the promise, 'We Will Rock You', is immediately followed by the joyous boast, 'We Are The Champions'. There was still some dross, though – could 'Sheer Heart Attack' really have been left off their third album? (Whether it had or not, it certainly didn't deserve a home on their *sixth*), and 'Sleeping On The Sidewalk' must be the worst boogie in a decade of bad boogies (apparently the group were just playing the song casually and didn't even realise the tapes were rolling). But the anthemic stuff really works, pro-

viding the perfect showcase for Freddie to strut his stuff around a stadium stage. The album reached number four in the UK.

Just before the album's release, Queen concluded their relationship with Trident completely, buying out the ongoing one per cent royalty they were due to pay as part of their severance agreement. They also agreed to a parting of the ways with manager John Reid (who found it virtually impossible to devote enough energies to both Queen *and* Elton John). Though the parting was on largely friendly terms, it was also costly – in addition to a (large) cash settlement, Queen also had to pay Reid a 15 per cent royalty in perpetuity on all the albums released to date. This being the second major management problem they'd encountered, the group determined now to look after their own affairs with help from Peter Brown (their day-to-day manager under Reid), tour manager Gerry Stickells, lawyer Jim Beach and his assistant Paul Prenter.

In November, they began their second US tour of the year. John Deacon showed up with a drastically short crew-cut, to ribald accusations from the others that he was 'going punk'. Later in the tour Deacon injured his hand (a post-party encounter with a plate glass window), and had to have nineteen stitches in the wound. In New York, Freddie met one of his heroines, Liza Minelli, and the band flew home in time for Christmas.

At the January 1978 MIDEM music business festival in Cannes, Queen picked up a French radio award for the 'rock band with the most potential' – not surprising, since 'We Will Rock You' had been at number one in France for over twelve weeks. It marked their breakthrough in that country.

Meanwhile, Queen continued to sort out the business side of their operations. They engaged a new accountant, Peter Chant, and with his help set up their own business company (Queen Productions Ltd), as well as their own music company (Queen Music Ltd) and film company (Queen Films Ltd). Chant took one look at their financial affairs, and advised his new clients that they should take their first 'year out' of the United Kingdom. (According to British tax law, if a person spends at least 300 days out of 365 out of the country, they don't have to pay any tax). Queen were about to become tax exiles.

QUEEN QUEEN QUEEN QUEEN QUEEN

JAZZ

Jazz

EMI EMA 788

Queen's new accountant Peter Chant also advised them to spread the recording sessions for their next album between two countries, so as to avoid falling under any one country's taxation laws – having sorted out their financial affairs in Britain, the last thing they needed was to fall foul of a foreign tax system. The arrangements for their 'year out' completed, Queen left Britain on April 9, 1978, for Stockholm, the first date of a two-month long European tour, which ended with four British gigs (two at Bingley Hall, Stafford, and two at Wembley's Empire Pool) in early May.

During this tour, Queen played West Berlin, and Roger Taylor and Brian May took the opportunity to cross through Checkpoint Charlie in the Berlin Wall and explore East Berlin. According to the group's official biography, it was an experience which moved them deeply. While there, Brian spotted some striking graffiti on the Berlin Wall: the word "Jazz" and a painting of a series of whirling concentric circles. May immediately felt strongly that these images fitted perfectly with the music they were planning to record. (Cream design would later produce the finished artwork for the album sleeve).

While in London for the Wembley gigs, Queen collected two awards: the readers of both the *Daily Mail* and the *Daily Mirror* had voted them the best British rock group. Shortly after the concerts, Roger Taylor and John Deacon flew to Switzerland to start work on recording at Mountain Studios. The other two members of Queen still had unfinished business in Britain before their exile could begin.

Brian May's wife Chrissie was pregnant with his first child, and the couple remained in the UK until after the birth of their son Jimmy on June 15 (John and Veronica Deacon had their

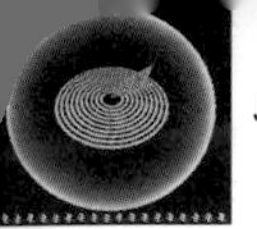

second son, Michael, in February). Brian then flew to Canada to celebrate his 31st birthday on July 19 with friends in Toronto, before heading for Switzerland to join the others. Freddie Mercury, meanwhile, stayed on in Britain to co-produce an album by a friend of his, actor Peter Straker, titled 'This One's On Me'. Freddie's co-producer for the album (in which he invested £20,000 of his own money) was Roy Thomas Baker, and possibly because of this reunion for the Straker project (or perhaps it was in itself a test-run of the Mercury-Baker relationship), Baker was asked to work with Queen once more for the 'Jazz' sessions. The recordings for 'Jazz', Queen's seventh studio album, took place between July and September 1978, commencing at Mountain Studios in Montreux, Switzerland and concluding at SuperBear studios in Nice in the south of France.

Baker's return may have been prompted by a lack of self-confidence. The group had failed to re-attain the critical heights of 'A Night At The Opera', and were dramatically at odds with current music fashion. And Queen did seem slightly lost: "We've saturated this multi-tracked album thing," said Mercury. "We want something different."

Something different is what they came up with. And if the album's strange mixture of disco, jazz, R&B and hard rock (not to mention the quasi-Islamic wailing on 'Mustapha') is occasionally meandering and messy, at other times, as on 'If You Can't Beat Them', it shows a determined joyousness; but for sheer bouncy verve, the singles taken from the album – 'Fat Bottomed Girls', 'Bicycle Race' and 'Don't Stop Me Now' – all take a lot of beating, and the album is worth checking out for May's gorgeously gentle 'Leaving Home Ain't Easy' alone.

The sessions had been far from uneventful. "Thunderbolt courtesy of God", reads one album credit, referring to the end of 'Dead On Time', which concludes with a roll of thunderclaps recorded by Brian May on a portable tape recorder during a violent thunderstorm at Montreux, which had cut off all power in the town. During recording the group fell in love with Montreux, a small, peaceful town on the shores of Lake Geneva, and enjoyed the experience of working at Mountain Studios – if you had to be an exile, there were worse places to be one.

The following year, the group received a

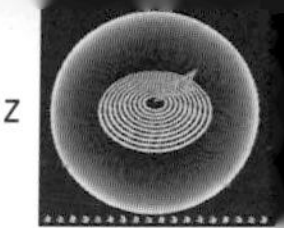

particularly painful tax demand from the British Inland Revenue, based on their past earnings. Queen's advisors decided that the taxman could wait – and the group accordingly used their money to buy Mountain Studios from its Dutch owners instead. When resident engineer David Richards asked them what they were going to do with the studio, Freddie cheerfully replied, "Throw it in the lake, dear – what do you think?"

Two more birthdays took place during recording, and enlivened the proceedings accordingly. On July 26 Roger Taylor turned 29, and held a huge party for jet set friends in a Montreux hotel, where Freddie Mercury startled guests by swinging from a huge chandelier. "I have *always* wanted to swing from a chandelier," Mercury confessed. "And when I saw this exquisite cut-crystal thing dangling there, I just could not resist it." By the time Freddie's 32nd birthday rolled around on September 5, recording had moved to sunny Nice, and his party involved much nude swimming (everybody but Freddie, according to reports), and Gilbert and Sullivan duets from Mercury and Peter Straker. While they were recording in Nice, the 'Tour De France' cycle race passed through the town – the inspiration for Freddie's 'Bicycle Race'.

Even before recording in Nice had finished, it was decided that the album's two most obviously commercial tracks – May's 'Fat Bottomed Girls' and Mercury's 'Bicycle Race' – should be released as a double 'A'-side single. To promote the record, some genius (conveniently, nobody can remember who, though the official explanation is that it was someone at the band's publicity company) decided that what was needed for the promotional video was a bevy of naked girls taking part in a bicycle race. If they'd known the trouble it would cause, they might have kept their mouth shut.

But at the time, it was generally thought to be a great idea. So, a call went out to all the well-known model agencies for girls who were not only willing to strip off, but could also ride bikes, and on September 17 sixty-five naked girls duly turned up at London's Wimbledon Stadium to be filmed by American video director Dennis De Vallance and a brace of stills photographers. Luckily for the girls, the weather was warm and sunny for the time of year. The bicycles were

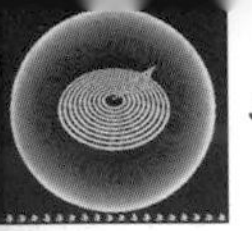

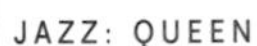

provided free of charge by cycle-manufacturers Halfords (who later refused to accept the return of the used saddles and made the band pay for replacements).

The results were used so discreetly in the video that one wonders why they bothered with the idea in the first place (other than for a cheap thrill on the day), the girls' nudity being almost completely obscured by solarisation and other special effects.

A colour photograph of the race was also featured on a poster included as an album insert (which was banned in the USA; instead an application form was enclosed, so that anyone who wanted the poster could write off for one), and a fairly innocuous rear view photo of one girl was used as the single sleeve and advertising poster. To the amazement of the band and their record company, when the single was released on October 13 the photo caused a public outcry, and later versions consequently feature the girl with a painted-on black bikini bottom (and in some versions, bra straps as well).

To the band the race, video and photos had almost certainly seemed like a bit of harmless, naughty-but-nice fun – certainly no worse than *The Sun*'s Page Three, which was virtually a national institution. But the press – especially the more politically aware pop press – thought otherwise, and accusations of sexploitation were hurled at the group. *NME* even ran a suitably unflattering rear-view picture of Mercury with the caption "Fat Bottomed Queen" (catty, or what?). Predictably, *NME* also hated the single: "They deserve all the vitriol that may be further hurled at them if this is an accurate preview of the new album." *Sounds* were kinder: "heavy, honeydripping, hard rock". But, as usual, the reviews scarcely mattered – 'Bicycle Race'/'Fat Bottomed Girls' reached number eleven on the British charts.

The group barely had time to notice all the fuss, as they flew directly from France to Dallas, Texas, where they opened their strenuous US tour (which lasted for the rest of the year) on October 28. Mind you, bringing naked girls on stage at Madison Square Garden during 'Bicycle Race' didn't exactly quieten the controversy...

Brian May later conceded that the nude cyclists may have been a bad move: "We lost some of our audience with that. 'How could

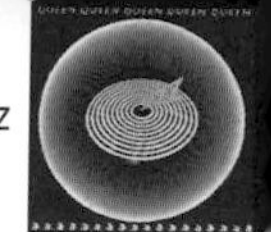

you do it? It doesn't go with your spiritual side.' But my answer is that the physical side is just as much a part of a person as the spiritual or intellectual side. It's fun. I'll make no apologies. All music skirts around sex, sometimes very directly. Ours doesn't. In our music, sex is either implied or referred to semi-jokingly, but it's always there."

Sex reared its head again at the launch party the band held for 400 guests to celebrate the album's release, at midnight on Hallowe'en in New Orleans: the entertainment comprised naked female mud-wrestlers, dwarfs, fire-eaters, steel bands, Zulu dancers, trad-jazz bands, voodoo dancers, strippers, drag artists and unicyclists (whether naked or not, we do not know). There were also some notorious groupies present, provided for the benefit of record company executives. Queen publicist Tony Brainsby flew in a planeload of British journalists for the party, and the subsequent story appeared in papers around the world.

Finally, on November 10, 'Jazz' was released in the UK, and the reviews were as bad as could be. "If you have a deaf relative, buy them this for Christmas," wrote *NME* while the *Sounds* reviewer commented, "I would dearly love to like Queen as much as I did in the early Seventies, but the task is becoming increasingly impossible." The public didn't care. The album went in at number two, and stayed on the charts for six months. By the time the next single – 'Don't Stop Me Now' – was released in January 1979, at least one critic was capable of being more objective: "Despite everything, Freddie has one of the best voices in rock, and Queen know how to change chords intelligently," *Record Mirror* admitted, before going on to ask, "Do they own EMI yet ?"

They didn't. But they were working on it.

QUEEN LIVE KILLERS

EMI EMSP 330

Queen kicked off 1979 with more touring: two months in Europe, and a month in Japan. All the dates on the European tour were recorded (using the Manor Mobile Studio) for a possible live album – though Queen still weren't all that keen on the idea, they were pressured into it by EMI, who wanted to stem the growing tide of live Queen bootlegs. So, immediately after the tour, Queen flew to Montreux to work on the live tapes with producer John Etchells.

The outcome was a *double* live album, 'Live Killers', featuring songs from sixteen different concerts. Despite the fact that the tapes had been given some cosmetic re-touching, the result is a live trot through Queen's back catalogue that suffers from duff sound, solos so tedious you'd think punk had never happened, and performances that were – at best – merely average. Freddie's dedication of 'Death On Two Legs' to former business associate Jack Nelson got bleeped out on legal grounds, and during most of 'Bohemian Rhapsody' the group were absent from the stage, while backing tapes played.

As May had earlier pointed out, "'Rhapsody' is not a stage number. A lot of people don't like us leaving the stage. But to be honest, I'd rather leave the stage than have us playing to a backing tape. If you're there and you've got backing tapes, it's a totally false situation. So we'd rather be upfront about it and say, 'Look, this is not something you can play on stage. It was multi-layered in the studio. We'll play it because we think you want to hear it'." This might be fair enough in a live context, with dry ice and an impressive lightshow to distract the attention... but why leave it on the album? Amazingly, the reviews were pretty kind, but Roger Taylor publicly disowned the whole thing.

It still managed to get to number three in the charts on its release in June 1979. That same month John and Veronica Deacon had their third child (a daughter, Laura), and Queen began work on their new studio album.

QUEEN

The Game

The Game

EMI EMA 795

Summer 1979 saw the group recording, mainly at Musicland Studios in Munich. There they discovered an unexpected asset in their engineer, Rheinhardt Mack (known simply as Mack). His ideas appealed to the group so much that they gave him a co-producer credit on the album, and he would work regularly with the group from now on.

That summer they also managed to fit in one stadium gig, at Saarbrucken in Germany... where, as Roger Taylor later recalled, his latest attempt at bleaching his hair blonde backfired somewhat: "It was bright, nauseating green. But it was too late to do anything about it, I just had to go on stage with it like that. It was so embarrassing, and Freddie took the piss all night."

And in October, Freddie finally got a chance to do ballet, when Wayne Eagling asked him to perform a dance piece as part of a Royal Ballet charity performance to raise money for mentally handicapped children. Eagling arranged Freddie's choreography, and he and another dancer, Derek Dane, helped him to exercise and rehearse. After several weeks' practice, Freddie appeared at the show at the London Coliseum, on October 7, performing dance interpretations of 'Bohemian Rhapsody' and a new song, 'Crazy Little Thing Called Love' (released two days earlier as the new Queen single). The ballet crowd responded enthusiastically to the event, which the rock press ignored completely.

'Crazy Little Thing Called Love' was a real departure: with its near rockabilly style it could have been covered by Elvis Presley. It was written by Freddie while in the bath ("I actually dragged an upright piano to my bedside once. I've been known to scribble lyrics in the middle of the night without putting the lights on.") Even the critics liked it, and it reached number two on the charts.

Though Elektra hadn't intended to release the song in the States, import copies of the single started to get substantial airplay on US radio stations – so much so that Elektra decided to take a chance and release it there after all. In February 1980, it went to number one there (as did the 'Game' album the following year).

May found the success the song brought them there a little bemusing: "We're not a singles group. We don't stake our reputation on singles and we never have done, but I think it's brought in a lot of younger people to our concerts." And the song may have achieved more than that, according to Roger Taylor: "It's not rockabilly exactly, but it did have that early Elvis feel, and it was one of the first records to exploit that. In fact, I read somewhere – in *Rolling Stone*, I think it was – that John Lennon heard it and it gave him the impetus to start recording again. If it's true – and listening to that last album it certainly sounds as if he explored similar influences – that's wonderful."

In November they set off on a British tour, and though they were still playing huge venues like Birmingham's NEC, this time the group were also deliberately playing smaller venues. May explained the logic behind the move: "We thought it was important to actually visit people again. Unless people can see you in their hometown, it can almost seem like you don't exist. It's also a relief to us because, having done the big barns, it's nice to be somewhere where people can actually see and hear you.

"The advantage of what we're doing this time is that, because our sound and light systems are better than ever, we can really knock audiences in the stomach. The only real disadvantage is that not everybody can get to see us – but I think that those who do have a much better time. It's great fun, too, because the reward is much more immediate and rewarding.

"In the larger venues you tend to lose that intimacy, but on the other hand you gain something else. You get a feeling of an event, and the more people there are, the greater the tension becomes. As a result, it makes you work harder, particularly to reach the people at the back.

"I doubt very much whether we'll be going back to large venues in England, because

there aren't actually many good ones. Bingley was quite good, but it's dirty and nasty for the people who come to watch. The NEC in Birmingham was the same – and it was definitely far too big.

"It's nice to do those sort of places once and see what they're like, but there aren't many we'd want to go back to. I wouldn't want to do Earl's Court again, nor Wembley, and it's quite possible that after doing Alexandra Palace we won't want to do that. But it's worth a try, because we're trying to do some special things with Ally Pally. We wanted to do one big gig in London to sweep up all the people we couldn't otherwise cover. We don't like to be artificially exclusive. I'd hate to get to the point where people who genuinely want to see us and who couldn't queue up for the tickets can't see us at all."

The British tour also featured Freddie's transition from Lurex to leather (trousers and peaked cap), and John Deacon's transition to collar and tie. Finally, they played a number of gigs in *ridiculously* small venues around the fringes of London: the 'Crazy Tour'. Nobody had thought Queen would ever set foot in Tottenham or Purley nightclubs, let alone play there. The logistics of organising it all were such that they caused tour manager Gerry Stickells to collapse from exhaustion. "The doctors told me to take it easy for a while," he later explained. "But none of them have ever been on the road with Queen. That advice is almost impossible to take. The tour might have been small in venue size, but it was a hassle. Some of the places were just so tiny that trying to cram in a band the size of Queen was nigh on impossible. But that's what they pay me for, working miracles. So we did it."

After their tour proper had finished, Queen finished off the year by playing one night of the benefit concerts for the people of Kampuchea on Boxing Day (the series of concerts also featured The Who, The Clash, Ian Dury, The Pretenders, The Specials, Rockpile with Robert Plant, and Elvis Costello... but despite the presence of Paul McCartney, the rumoured Beatles reunion once again failed to take place). Queen's whole set was recorded but only one track – 'Now I'm Here' – was released on the official live album of the event.

January 25, 1980, saw the release of 'Save Me', which reached number 11 on the charts

despite the reviews ("Tat music from a tat band," said *NME*.) Meanwhile, 'Crazy Little Thing Called Love' was racing up the charts worldwide. Apart from its success Stateside, the song also went to number one in Canada, Mexico, Holland, New Zealand and Australia.

February to May was spent at Musicland Studios in Munich, finishing the recording of 'The Game'. Mercury made a return visit to Britain to appear (as a favour) on Kenny Everett's TV show, and while in London bought an eight-bedroomed Victorian mansion (complete with garden) in the middle of Kensington for £500,000 (he paid *cash*). Freddie eventually carried out extensive alterations to the property, furnishing it with Japanese antiques... but it took over four years before he moved in. "Every person who makes a lot of money has a dream he wants to carry out, and I achieved that dream with this wonderful house," he later said. "Whenever I watched Hollywood movies set in plush homes with lavish decor, I wanted that for myself, and now I've got it. But to me it was much more important to get the damn thing than to actually go and live in it. Maybe the challenge has worn off now. I'm very much like that – once I get something I'm not that keen on it any more. I still love the house, but the real enjoyment is that I've achieved it.

"Sometimes, when I'm alone at night, I imagine that when I'm 50 I'll creep into that house as my refuge, and then I'll start making it a home. Anyways, as it is I can only spend sixty days a year in England for tax reasons."

The album was released in June, a few days after the 'Play The Game' single (which reached number fourteen). The cover photos revealed a new image for the group – all of them (except May) now sported much shorter hair, and Freddie had even grown a bushy moustache. Adopting a look that was synonymous with the macho gay stereotype may well have cost Queen mileage with American rock fans more used to seeing heavy rockers with long hair, and it didn't go down that well with long-time Queen supporters either – the band's offices were inundated with razor blades sent in by fans. The single was trashed by *NME* ("Another three minutes of indulgent, over-produced trivia, just like I expected"), as was the album ("old and tired and bland and blinkered").

And that's a pretty fair assessment (apart from the singles); despite the two-year lay-off between studio albums, it seemingly hadn't resulted in greater inspiration, and most of this offering is self-indulgent drivel – not so much filler as stodge. That the album featured the group's first use of a synthesizer is perhaps indicative of their desire to move on, but also perhaps of their lack of a clear direction to move *in*. John Deacon later defended the decision to use them saying, "We wanted to experiment with all that new studio equipment. We had always been keen to try out anything new or different whilst recording. The synthesizers then were so good, they were very advanced compared to the early Moogs, which did little more than make a series of weird noises. The ones we were using could duplicate all sorts of sounds and instruments – you could get a whole orchestra out of them at the touch of a button. Amazing." 'The Game' album went to number one, and achieved gold status.

But despite the album's shortcomings, the singles were – once again – all ace: the hepcat rockabilly of 'Crazy Little Thing Called Love', the plaintive, poignant 'Save Me' (a song genuinely touching in retrospect)... and the track released halfway through the three-month long US tour that Queen began on July 1, John Deacon's (heavily) Chic-influenced 'Another One Bites The Dust' (which only reached number seven in the UK., but which hit the top of the rock, disco *and* soul charts in the States). As Deacon later recalled: "I listened to a lot of soul music when I was in school, and I've always been interested in that sort of music. I'd been wanting to do a track like 'Another One Bites The Dust' for a while, but originally all I had was the line and the bass riff. Gradually I filled it in and the band added ideas. I could hear it as a song for dancing, but had no idea it would become as big as it did. The song got picked up off our album and some of the black radio stations in the US started playing it, which we've never had before." The song would later be sampled by Grandmaster Flash.

The US tour concluded with four sold-out nights at Madison Square Garden, then the group took a holiday for most of October, before returning to the studio to finish recording a project they'd started during the 'Game' sessions – their first film soundtrack.

ORIGINAL SOUNDTRACK MUSIC BY QUEEN

Flash Gordon

EMI EMC 3351

Several years previously, Queen had been approached to write and perform a theme tune for director Mike Hodges' $22 million remake of the adventures of the 1930's science-fiction serial-hero Flash Gordon. When Queen were first mooted for the job producer Dino DeLaurentis (who had allegedly never heard a rock group before) supposedly asked, "Who are the Queens ?"

In the end, they provided not just the theme tune, but the entire movie soundtrack. As May later explained: "We saw twenty minutes of the finished film and thought it very good and over the top... We wanted to do something that was a *real* soundtrack... It's a first in many ways, because a rock group hasn't done this type of thing before, or else it's been toned down and they've been asked to write mushy background music, whereas we were given the licence to do what we liked, as long as it complemented the picture."

The project was recorded hurriedly between touring, using different studios and dovetailing with the final sessions for The Game, and the final sessions began in October 1980 at Anvil Studios in England. Taylor also found time to play drums on Gary Numan's album 'Dance', which was recorded in London around the same time.

They finished recording in November, just before leaving on a tour of Europe and the UK (all stadium gigs), and later that month released a single from soundtrack – 'Flash' – the movie's theme (it reached number ten).

The album was released on December 8, just as the British leg of the tour was climaxing with three nights at Wembley Arena. The following night, as a tribute to John Lennon (assassinated that day), Queen performed a moving version of 'Imagine'.

Around this time, Brian May talked about

Queen's audience, and the pressures of performing: "We do have a lot of power. We just hope we can divert it in the right direction... I know it looks like a Nuremberg rally, but our fans are sensible people. They're creating the situation as much as we are, it's not that we're leading them like sheep... You just play music which excites people, which interests them. It's rock 'n' roll - there's no philosophical reason why we should be there... Touring is certainly the most immediately fulfilling part of what we do, and it's not really a big strain - mentally or physically – because we're well organised, we know how to do it. All you have to worry about is playing well on the night. For me, it's by far the best part of being in the band. Suddenly, life becomes simple again!"

May also reflected on the group's decade-long love-hate relationship with the UK music press: "There are lots of little mechanisms built into the relationships between a musician and the press, which means – almost inevitably – that you fall out. But it happened very early to us, so perhaps it doesn't apply. Generally, I could write the reviews of our albums, the good ones and the bad ones... It's a very limited view of what goes on: as soon as something becomes successful, it can't be worth anything... I did think in the beginning it was important to keep the lines of communication open, to talk to everybody. In the end though, after many experiences, you find that it really doesn't come out. If the guy has stated already that he hates you, and can't see anything in you that is worthwhile, then nine times out of ten, if you spend your time trying to convince him how good you are, he goes away and writes what he thought anyway! We do have a reputation for not wanting to talk to people, which is really not that true most of the time – if we have time, we'll always talk. But if someone slags you off in a way you don't think is fair, you don't want to talk to them again."

And talked about Queen's growing success: "You're progressing when you get to play Madison Square Garden for one night, then two, then three. You're reaching more people each time, and it's a recognition that the people who enjoyed themselves the first time have come back and brought their friends. It's a good feeling, to build all the time. It doesn't mean that in some ways you're not conscious it's not an artificial aim – getting bigger is not the be-all and

end-all. Often if you sell more records, it doesn't mean that the quality of the record is any better."

Indeed. To be fair, Queen's first original movie soundtrack works brilliantly as an accompaniment to the visuals (i.e. it's just as camp as the film). On its own, however, it's (a) repetitious and (b) pretty dull: 35 minutes of variations on a theme, punctuated by sound effects and dialogue from Max Von Sydow and the rest of the cast. (On the plus side, at least you get to hear the group playing the Wedding March.)

A planned 'Greatest Hits' compilation was shelved when it was decided to promote 'Flash Gordon' as an official Queen album (to mixed critical reaction, it must be said). It still reached number ten, and went gold. By the end of 1980, Queen had sold a total of 45 million albums and 25 million singles, and the group finished the year achieving an entry in 'The Guinness Book Of Records': they were listed as the highest-paid company directors in Britain.

QUEEN
GREATEST HITS

Greatest Hits

EMI EMTV 30

In February 1981 Queen set off for Japan, where they played five nights at Tokyo's Budokan (and a Tokyo department store closed its doors to the public so Freddie could shop in peace). Then they did something almost unheard of: they headed for South America, for six dates in Argentina and two in Brazil (nicknamed the 'Tour Of A Million No Problems!'), which culminated in Queen playing to an audience of 251,000 at São Paulo's Morumbi Stadium. These countries were virtually virgin territory for rock (other than via pirate tapes), and Queen were the first major rock act to tour there. They did so in style, flying in twenty tons of sound equipment from their Japanese tour, a further forty ton load from Miami (including a full football field covering of artificial turf, to protect the playing fields in the arenas they were due to play), plus another sixteen tons (and what do you get?) of stage scaffolding from Los Angeles. The tour took nine months to organise, and with estimated running costs of £25,000 per day, even despite the high ticket prices no one could accuse the group of just doing it for the money. There were a zillion problems each day, and much Latin madness, but the challenge paid off (a total concert gross of $30 million), and the audiences (a total of 479,000, plus a South American TV audience of 35 million for the telecast of the first Argentinian gig) were among the most enthusiastic the group had ever seen.

"We were really nervous," Freddie later confessed. "We had no right to automatically expect the works from an alien territory. I don't think they'd ever seen such an ambitious show, with this lighting and effects."

May confirmed: "It's a long time since we've felt such warmth from a new audience, although we couldn't see much because of the size of the crowd. We feel really good about it now, as if our ambitions have been

partly realised again."

But Queen were also accused of political naïveté, and were slagged off by the Western press for visiting areas deemed politically unsound. It wouldn't be the last time. Queen – who considered themselves to be apolitical musicians – were forced to confront the dubious politics of the countries they visited, notably in Argentina. When the group were invited to meet President Viola of Argentina, only Roger Taylor refused to accept the invitation. Later that year, he commented: "In a way I was surprised that we didn't get more criticism for playing South America. I didn't think we were being used as tools by political régimes, although obviously you have to co-operate with them. We were playing for the people. We didn't go there with the wool pulled over our eyes. We fully know what the situation is like in some of those countries, but for a time we made thousands of people happy. Surely that must count for something?

"We weren't playing for the government, we were playing to lots of ordinary Argentinian people. In fact, we were asked to meet the President, President Viola, and I refused. Didn't want to meet him, because that would have been playing into their hands. We went there to do some rock music for the people."

Asked whether there was anywhere else exotic that Queen would like to visit, Taylor replied, "I wouldn't mind playing Russia at some time. But over there you have to be carefully vetted by the government. The Russian authorities like Cliff Richard and Elton John, but Queen are still considered a little bit wild."

Throughout the controversy, Mercury maintained a press silence. As May commented: "Freddie doesn't talk any more because he's a little tired of Queen and himself being misrepresented. I think anybody who meets Freddie would be in for a bit of a surprise. He's not quite the prima donna you'd imagine. Obviously, he's a positive character, but so are we all. When all is said and done he works damned hard and puts on a good show."

In April Roger Taylor released his first solo album, 'Fun In Space', which he'd recorded during a six-week period in Switzerland the previous year. "The title 'Fun In Space' doesn't mean that the album should be regarded as 'Son Of Flash Gordon'," Taylor insisted, "but in many ways it is nostalgic, cap-

turing the old days when life was perhaps a little more uncertain. I've got some old sci-fi books and magazines which I browse through from time to time. Maybe there are things up there in space watching us. I wouldn't find that surprising at all."

Recording this album (during a period when the other Queen members were quite sensibly resting and relaxing) had been a draining experience for Taylor, but a necessary one: "Afterwards I was so mentally exhausted that I couldn't even be trusted to select the single. There were certain things I wanted to do which weren't within the Queen format; in a way it's like flushing out your system, and until you've done it you just don't feel fulfilled. If I get more ideas for songs I might eventually do another solo thing, but Queen would always get priority." Despite a critical thrashing ("a rich man's self-indulgence run riot" said *Melody Maker*), the album reached a respectable number sixteen.

On May 22, Brian and Chrissy May had another child (a daughter, Louisa), after which Brian flew to Montreux, where recording sessions for the next studio album, 'Hot Space', had already begun.

In September Freddie celebrated his 34th birthday by flying all his closest friends to New York (by Concorde) for a mega-party (it lasted five days) at the Berkshire Hotel. Then, after rehearsing in New Orleans, Queen returned to South America for another tour (dubbed the 'Gluttons For Punishment' tour) – this time playing concerts in Venezuela and Mexico. Again, there were manic problems: in Venezuela, two shows had to be cancelled when Venezuelan President Ethancourt died and the country was plunged into official mourning, and in Mexico the group fled the country after only two shows – basically because (a) it was doubtful they'd get paid, and (b) the security for the shows was non-existent, and Mexican fans tended to express their appreciation by throwing large (and possibly lethal) items of rubbish on stage. Queen decided to quit while they still could.

In November 1981 Queen celebrated their first decade together with a 'Greatest Hits' compilation, the release of which had been delayed nearly a year so as to make room for 'Flash Gordon'. But it was worth the wait: seventeen tracks, and not a dud in sight. The ret-

QUEEN
GREATEST HITS

rospective proved that, while their albums had been patchy and padded, Queen's status as one of the great pop singles bands of the last twenty years was (and is) beyond doubt. About the only thing that would have improved this collection would have been the inclusion of a couple of extra tracks ('Keep Yourself Alive' and 'Tie Your Mother Down' are two that spring to mind). "Class all the way through," said *Record Mirror*, and the public obviously agreed – the album went straight to number one, and spent six months during its (initial) run on the charts. It would return to the charts on more than one occasion.

A month earlier, Queen had released 'Greatest Flix', a video compilation which contained the promo videos for all their singles, plus a film of 'Killer Queen' made especially for this compilation. And they didn't stop there, either - there was a book as well, 'Queen's Greatest Pix' (published by Quartet), which – like the album and the video compilation – featured a cover portrait of the group taken by Lord Snowdon. The book was a compilation of photographs old and new, with reprints of articles written by Paul Gambaccini, Ray Coleman and others. The photos were selected by former White House photographer Jacques Lowe (who sifted through over 3,000 photographs of the group before making his final choice). A rival book published at the same time (by Judith Davis, published by Proteus) was unsuccessfully injuncted by the group. Queen were annoyed – they'd tried to stop the book, not because of sour grapes at anything Davis had written, but because the Proteus book carried a claim on its cover to be 'official', which it wasn't.

Freddie summed up their feelings at having survived the first ten years: "As long as we feel a sense of achievement and that we are breaking new ground – like doing the South American tours, and planning something like the Far East – we're happy, and we ought to continue."

QUEEN

Hot Space

Hot Space

EMI EMTA 797

A month before 'Greatest Hits' came out, Queen released the single which became their second British number one – 'Under Pressure', a collaboration with David Bowie. Queen had been recording in Montreux, where Bowie lived, and one day he dropped in on the recording sessions. Roger Taylor was ecstatic about the results: "It's one of the very best things Queen have ever done, and it happened so casually, when David simply visited us at our studio in Montreux. As long as we can continue to do this, and surprise even ourselves, we'll carry on."

Bowie himself was more reserved about the song (which was originally titled 'People On Streets': "They turned up in Montreux, so I went down to the studio and we just started one of those inevitable jams, which led to a skeleton of a song. I thought it was quite a nice tune, so we finished it off. It sort of half came off, but I think it could have been a lot better. It was a rush thing, one of those things that took place over twenty-four hours. I think it stands up better as a demo. It was done so quickly that some of it (the lyric) makes me cringe a bit, but the idea I like." The initial sessions were finished off (by Roger, Freddie and Bowie) in New York.

In November 1981 Queen also played two concerts in Montreal which were filmed by the Canadian company MobileVision for a planned 'in concert' feature film. The following month, the group flew to Munich, to finish the new album. As May later explained, "Munich had a huge effect on all our lives. Because we spent so much time there, it became almost another home, and a place in which we lived different lives. It was different from being on tour, where there would be an intense contact with a city for a couple of days, and then we would move on. In Munich we all became embroiled

in the lives of the local people. We found ourselves inhabiting the same clubs for most of the night, most nights! The Sugar Shack in particular held a fascination for us. It was a rock disco with an amazing sound system, and the fact that some of our records *didn't* sound very good in there made us change our whole perspective on our mixes and our music.

"'Another One Bites The Dust' and 'Dragon Attack' on the 'Game' album both showed a trend towards more 'rhythmic' rock. And 'Hot Space' became almost totally oriented that way. Freddie in particular was keen to explore that avenue to the extreme! ('Body Language', 'Staying Power' etc). The multi-track of 'Staying Power' was sent to Arif Mardin in the US (famous for Aretha Franklin, Chaka Khan productions, etc.) and he put a live horn section on using his own arrangement. This was a very different approach for us.

"In retrospect it's probably true to say that our efficiency in Munich was not very good. Our social habits made us generally start work late in the day, feeling tired, and (for me especially, and perhaps for Freddie) the emotional distractions became destructive."

While recording the album, Freddie and Roger guested (backing vocals) on a track by Billy Squier; later that Spring, Taylor also guested (drums) on Gary Numan's 'Dance' album, which was being recorded in London. After completing 'Hot Space', the band managed to grab a few days' holiday in LA, before setting off on their next tour.

And they toured virtually non-stop from April through to November – a jaunt that took in Europe, Britain, North America and Japan. To help reproduce the album's feel in a live context, the group recruited a keyboards player, Morgan Fisher (ex-Mott). On April 19 they released 'Body Language', the next single from the album, but it only reached number twenty-five (nor did it do well in the States, where MTV banned the video on account of its liberal use of naked flesh and baby oil).

In late April, at the start of Britain's conflict with Argentina over the Falklands/Malvinas, Queen were at number one in Argentina with 'Under Pressure'. The Argentinian government promptly banned the group from ever playing there again, and banished their music from the radio for the duration of hostilities.

"He was so vain, but we tolerated it - everyone did. It was part of him, part of his character. He just wouldn't have been Freddie without that vanity."

Helen McConnell

QUEEN

The 'Hot Space' album was released on May 21, to (for once) favourable response from the critics. May had described the record as "an attempt to do funk properly", but while it definitely has one foot on the dance floor, much of it still sounds like wimpy white disco. But long-time Queen fans (and radio DJs) generally didn't care for it; like Brian May, they were unhappy that synthesizers overshadowed May's guitar. Despite the fact that it sold reasonably well, (it got to number four), Deacon later admitted that the band were "disappointed" with the album. Still, Taylor's compressed drum sound has been much sampled over the years, the collaboration with Bowie remains a *tour de force* and the poppier moments echo the best parts of Queen's earlier work with a new-found energy.

When the tour reached England at the end of May, Queen played Leeds United football ground ("One of our best gigs ever," according to May). Plans to play Manchester's Old Trafford and London's Arsenal football grounds had to be scrapped due to lack of toilet facilities (Britain's entire stockpile of chemical toilets had been booked elsewhere, for the official visit of Pope John Paul II). So the London concert was moved to the Milton Keynes Bowl, where the show was recorded (and later broadcast) by Tyne Tees TV. May later recalled that: "None of us thought it was a very good gig at the time – we were wishing they had filmed Leeds. I particularly found it hard to get the sound right, and couldn't hear the monitors very well. But Tyne Tees filmed it, and mixed it themselves, with no help from

us; and we now think it's one of the better videos of our live shows. 'Staying Power', especially, sounds even tighter than the record (and heavier)." The group had made the journey from London to Milton Keynes by helicopter, an experience Freddie felt he could have lived without: "I was terrified. I don't like flying in anything smaller than a jumbo jet, darling, and this thing was so *small*! But I was told we had photographers and the like at the other end waiting for us to arrive, so I couldn't possibly let them see how shaken I was! My knuckles were white from gripping the arm rests. But when we arrived I stepped out of that machine with a smile on my face looking like I did it every day; no one was any the wiser."

Brian's balladic 'Las Palabras De Amor (The Words Of Love)' was released as the next single at the start of June. The media leapt on the fact that this was a Spanish language song, and in the light of Queen's experience of Argentina Freddie was asked to comment on the Falklands war: "It's our young men killing their young men. There's no glory in being blown to bits." Sensible words, but they didn't endear him to the gung-ho jingoistic tabloids. This single reached number seventeen, and the next ('Back Chat', released in August), only got to number forty.

On the North American leg of the tour (which featured Fred Mandell on keyboards), Taylor took time out to sing backing vocals on three tracks of Kansas's album 'Vinyl Confessions'. Queen also got to fly on Elvis Presley's private plane, the *Lisa Marie*, and parted company with their American label, Elektra, signing with EMI for those territories previously covered under the Elektra deal.

Having spent the better part of a year on the road, Queen decided they deserved a holiday. In 1983, they were going to take a year off. This naturally fuelled media speculation that they were on the verge of breaking up, which the group denied. They also made it clear they were sticking together for creative reasons, and not just commercial ones. "It's not a question of money any more," said Freddie. "I spend money like it's nothing. You know, I could be penniless tomorrow, but I'd get it back somehow." Taylor was more candid: "We just don't want to be seen to fail. That's what keeps us going."

QUEEN THE WORKS

The Works

EMI EMC 2400141

Queen really needed a year off, to refresh themselves musically and personally, as Taylor later admitted: "After touring America, Europe and Japan we were totally knackered, so we thought we deserved a bit of a rest... It also had a lot to do with the last album not doing as well as previous LPs. We realised that it hadn't been what a lot of fans wanted or expected from us, so we thought a break would give us the opportunity to think things through a bit."

But that didn't mean they weren't active...

Back at Musicland in Munich, Freddie had begun work on a solo album. He'd also been approached by Giorgio Moroder, who had acquired the rights to Fritz Lang's silent science-fiction movie, 'Metropolis', and intended to release it in a new colourised form with a rock soundtrack. Freddie ended up contributing one song, 'Love Kills'. For a time Moroder's version of 'Metropolis' was the only one available on video; anyone with a shred of sensitivity watched it with the colour and the sound switched off (no offence, Freddie). The song reached number two in the UK when it was released as a single the following year (it was kept off the top slot by Frankie Goes To Hollywood's 'Relax' – an unstoppable hit that year, though some of us could never work out why).

John Deacon, meanwhile, played bass on 'Picking Up Sounds', a single by Man Friday And Jive Junior. Deacon also jammed with various musician friends (and would-be musicians, like tennis players John McEnroe and Vitas Gerulaitas), and played with Taylor on sessions for the latter's second solo album.

In April 1983 Brian May flew to LA, with vague plans for recording a solo project (his guitar flew in the seat next to him. It paid child's fare). In the end, he called a bunch of musician friends, and the project turned into a star jam session, recorded at LA's Record

Plant and featuring Eddie Van Halen, bassist Phil Chen and REO-Speedwagon drummer Alan Gratzer. The result was 'Star Fleet', a single based on the theme to a children's puppet show that was big on Japanese TV (and highly popular with May's son). It was followed by a mini-album, 'Fleet Project', released that October, at which time May talked about the project: "To be honest, I didn't even know if I could play with other musicians – I had been *so* with Queen. I thought, 'What kind of a musician am I ?' I had been working the machine, but maybe I had become too much of a slave to it... Edward and I took a break from recording, and started talking about how it was in the old days, when Eric Clapton was doing his thing with John Mayall. We all found the 'Beano' album had been a big influence on us. Remember, the one with Eric reading the comic on the cover? It was a classic collector's item for every guitarist. It sounded like they were having so much fun they couldn't stop... 'Blues Breaker', which takes up all of Side two on the album, is my favourite part of the record. It seemed very indulgent, putting out a long jam but, having listened to it, I think it's worthwhile... It's rock blues, with all the mistakes left in."

Freddie Mercury was also hobnobbing with other rock stars in LA – specifically Michael Jackson. Freddie and Michael recorded two songs together at Jackson's home studio, for possible release on Freddie's album and/or the next Jackson album. But the songs didn't work out as well as they'd hoped, and both parties agreed not to release them (in 1993, Queen aides were denying the tracks existed at all). The following year Mercury told an interviewer, "I'd like to release something with Michael because he is a really marvellous person to work with. It's all a question of time, because we never seem to be together at the same time. Just think, I could have been on 'Thriller' – think of the royalties I've missed out on.

"Michael has been a friend of ours for a long time. He's been to our shows and enjoyed them. We make a great team."

Only Roger Taylor seemed at a loose end that summer. He was arrested for drunkenness at Monaco Grand Prix, fined heavily and ordered to leave the principality. A few months later he took part in a powerboat race

in Dorset, and the boat he was helping to man came in second (a fellow crew member was Gary Numan).

Brian May's other solo projects included playing guitar on Jeffrey Osborne's single, 'Two Wrongs Don't Make A Right', and also co-producing (with Mack) the début album by Heavy Pettin', 'Letting Loose' (recorded in London and Munich). Continuing the heavy metal theme, May also jammed live with Def Leppard at a concert at the LA Forum: "I was bowled over by them. Just amazing. Their show was one of the highest energy things I've *ever* seen. I was turned on to them by Heavy Pettin'. They destroyed the place. I went back and told 'em so, and they invited me to play with them the next night. I was highly flattered, so I went on and played a song with them at the end, which was great fun."

In the end, Queen didn't even manage a whole year off. That July Freddie and John met with film director Tony Richardson to discuss the possibility of Queen providing soundtrack music for his next movie, an adaptation of John Irving's *The Hotel New Hampshire*. Fired with enthusiasm, Queen entered LA's Record Plant the following month to begin recording. But it soon became evident that the new material wouldn't be right for a film; reluctantly, they abandoned the idea, and concentrated on making a new studio album. A projected South American tour had fallen through, leaving them free to give the recording their all, literally, to 'The Works'.

Brian May later talked about their time apart: "We were getting too close to each other... getting on each other's nerves, which happens periodically. This time we said, 'Let's take a break and give ourselves some breathing space. Let's do individual things, then we can come back to Queen when we actually feel motivated.' We took about five months off work, up until August this year.

"During that time we met and talked a lot, but we didn't actually do anything. We wanted the next album we made to be in a new situation. We were trying to break from our old record company in America, which was important. We didn't want to deliver another album in that situation."

He admitted that it cost them $3 million to buy their way out of their US deal with Elektra, and re-sign with EMI's sister company Capitol;

and also that they hadn't wanted to put out anything substandard: "There was that feeling that we might just be making another Queen album and putting it back into the machine. We didn't want that, and it's all worked out very well. We agreed on Capitol, and signed with them. Suddenly, we have a company in America that's really *excited* to be getting their first Queen album."

May also discussed the friction within the group: "There's always been a lot of tension within Queen, because we don't like the same things as far as music is concerned and have to find common ground. We often disagree about how things should be presented. We're all very forthright and different. We are very stubborn, but there is a democracy – nobody has a bigger share of the say than anybody else. But sometimes it's very tense and very hard.

"It's not the touring, though. That's the best and easiest part. You have to go out there and be as good as you damn well can be. But the thought of doing another album just didn't appeal to us after the last tour, so we thought it was no use forcing it. Better to wait until we'd something to offer.

"We didn't want to split up because we felt that's a mistake so many people have made, from The Beatles onwards. It would have been so good if they could have held together for longer. No matter how talented the individuals are, the group is always something more than its components. And we think Queen is an example of a proper group. With all its shortcomings, I think it's worth keeping together.

"After all the fights we still tend to come up with things that have been through the sieve and are worthwhile - *because* of all the fighting. We still care. I think our new album is damn good, much better than anything we've done for a while. It's going to be called 'The Works'. And it really is! There's all the Queen trademarks – lots of production, arrangements and harmonies.

"We've experimented a lot in the past, and some of the experiments didn't work. Our last album was one big experiment, and a lot of people totally hated it. And it didn't sell very well – not compared to earlier stuff, anyway. We've had ups and downs. People don't realise that. They think Queen can't do anything wrong.

"People think we can just stick out an album and it's easy for us. But really it's not. There are varying degrees of success, and we are always conscious that our next album may also be our last. We don't like to repeat ourselves, so there is always the chance that people will hate what we do.

"It's funny... everyone thought Queen had this big master plan to conquer the world, but really we were so excited *just* to make an album – that was the ambition in itself. None of us knew what was ahead."

Mercury also dismissed ideas of a break-up: "I used to think we'd go on for five years, but it's got to the point where we're all actually too *old* to break up. Can you imagine forming a new band at 40? Be a bit silly, wouldn't it?" And the rumours of a split were certainly nothing new, as May pointed out: "People have been rumouring that Queen are going to split up for the last eight years at least. I've got some great cuttings at home from people saying, 'One thing is certain – Queen will no longer exist in a year's time'. And that was in 1973!"

Queen's low-profile year ended with the birth of John and Veronica Deacon's fourth child, Joshua.

1984 saw the band active once again. At the end of January, they released a new single, 'Radio Ga-Ga', written by Taylor: "One day the radio came on in my house and my three-year-old son Felix came out with, 'radio poo-poo!' I thought that sounded good, so I changed it around a bit and came up with 'Radio Ga Ga'. The song came after I'd locked myself in a studio for three days with a synthesizer and a drum machine."

One can't help but feel that 'radio poo-poo' was a more accurate description of the state of British broadcasting, though. Taylor also explained how the video for the song came to feature footage from 'Metropolis', incorporated into the group's own (pretty lavish) scenario: "Giorgio Moroder had bought the film rights to 'Metropolis', and he wanted us to write a song to go with it. We wrote him a song, and we swapped it for the rights to some footage from the film. It's a great movie, and I'd always been interested in using images from it... there's a sense of nostalgia in watching a silent film that links in with the nostalgic view of radio I got from remembering nights spent listening to Radio Luxembourg under

the bedclothes." Another version has it that Queen bought the 'Metropolis' footage directly from the German government! The song was infectious enough ("arrogant nonsense," said *NME*) to get to number two in Britain, and to number one in nineteen other countries.

"It's not the money any more," said Taylor. "It's the thought of, 'Christ, what would we do if we ended it?' Obviously, we could all have our solo careers and put new bands together, but that would be like climbing Mount Everest again. Queen is what we do; it's what we're used to. But we'll only do it while the enthusiasm's there. The more interest that's shown in the band, the more enthusiasm is generated within the band – that's why it's been such a thrill that 'Radio Ga Ga' is such a big hit. Obviously, if people stopped buying our records and coming to our live shows, we'd knock it on the head pretty quickly."

In February Queen played the San Remo Song Festival in Italy, where Taylor and May argued about material, the stage and a thousand other things. Freddie managed to crack them up laughing, which saved the day (and possibly the band). One of the other acts playing the festival was Culture Club, and Freddie later commented on Boy George: "He's a great talent. That boy is so brave. When I started off, rock bands were all wearing jeans, and suddenly here's Freddie Mercury in a Zandra Rhodes frock with make-up and black nail varnish. It was totally outrageous. In a way, Boy George has just updated that thing, the whole glam-rock bit. George is more like a drag queen. It's the same outrage, just doubled." Mercury was also asked about his relationship with Michael Jackson, and said, "Michael Jackson and I have grown apart a bit since his massive success with 'Thriller'. He's simply retreated into a world of his own. Two years ago, we used to have great fun going to clubs together, but now he won't come out of his fortress. It's very sad. He's so worried that someone will do him in that he's paranoid about absolutely everything."

Later that month *The Sun* newspaper ran an interview with Freddie Mercury, hooked around the 'admission', "Oh yes, I'm gay. I've done all that." Mercury's response was remarkably restrained: "I was completely misquoted. But from the beginning, the press have always written whatever they wanted

about Queen, and they can get away with it. The woman who wrote that story wanted a total scoop from me and didn't get anything. I said, 'What do you want to hear? That I deal cocaine?' But for God's sake, if I wanted to make big confessions about my sex life, would I go to *The Sun*, of all papers, to do it? There's no fucking way I'd do that. I'm too intelligent."

'The Works' was released on February 27. Two years had gone by between albums; this time the accent was on pop (of the nine tracks on the album, four were released as singles) and a more obviously Queen-like sound.

At Roger Taylor's girlfriend Dominique's suggestion, the group dressed up in drag for the video to the next single, 'I Want To Break Free'. The idea was to do a send-up of 'Coronation Street', and the finished article is one of Queen's finest moments – pure tongue-in-cheek high camp from Freddie, in mini-skirt and moustache. But the cross-dressing proved too much for MTV (who probably didn't get the humour), and the video was banned in several US States. As Taylor later commented, "We had done some really serious, epic videos in the past, and we just thought it was time we had some fun. We wanted people to know that we didn't take ourselves too seriously, that we could still laugh at ourselves. I think we proved that." (The song was released as a single in April, and reached number three on the UK charts.)

Other notable tracks on the album were May's anti-nuke 'Hammer To Fall', which – like much of Queen's *next* album – would feature in the soundtrack of the movie *Highlander*. The album's anti-suicide song (a recurring theme for Queen) was 'Keep Passing The Open Windows', which had survived from the abandoned film project – the title being a quote from John Irving's novel *The Hotel New Hampshire*.

Though 'The Works' didn't fare any better in the States than 'Hot Space' had done, it still became Queen's biggest album to date, its sales beaten only by that of the 'Greatest Hits' collection. May was proud of it: "I always got the most enjoyment out of the harder material. Actually, our new album is a lot harder... but I did fight to get it that way. We've done some fantastic over-the-top harmonies and a lot of heavy things that we haven't done for years."

"The pressure has always been against me, because not everyone in the band is into the same stuff as I am. I get the most pleasure out of things that I can hammer down and get some excitement out of. Basically, I'm like a little boy with the guitar – I just love the fat, loud sound of it. But that's not important to the others, and I agree with this: the songs come first. That's where the common ground ends and the arguments begin. The result is always a compromise."

John and Roger undertook a promotional tour of Australia and the Far East (112 interviews in sixteen days!), before heading off for a much needed brief holiday. May guested on a track for the new Billy Squier album, while Mercury was recording his solo album in Munich.

In May the group played the Golden Rose Festival in Montreux, despite their irritation at having to mime for the TV cameras, as Roger (who squeezed in some solo recording while in Montreux) later explained: "All events like that are farces, 'cause you're miming to playback, but Freddie made that pretty obvious. But, 400 million viewers... who could say 'no'?" Taylor's next solo single, 'Man On Fire' was released in June, as was Taylor's second solo album, 'Strange Frontier'. Apart from cover versions of songs by Dylan and Springsteen, the album also included one song co-written with Mercury, and one co-written with Rick Parfitt of Status Quo. It got unanimously trashed by the critics (*Sounds* called it, "The product of a talented guy with no reason to do anything ever again. Empty.").

Brian May, meanwhile, had sanctioned Guild Guitars of New York to make replicas of his 'Red Special' homemade guitar: "They've been through the guitar, taken it to pieces and measured it up, and they reckon they can make something which is very close to the one I made myself all those years ago. Now, hopefully, there should be a Brian May guitar which sounds like my one." The Guild copy (the BHM1) was launched in June 1984, but the price – £1,200 – proved prohibitive. When Guild wanted to make a cheaper version by cutting a few corners, May withdrew his support.

In July 'It's A Hard Life' was released as a single (it reached number six in the UK). That month they also began rehearsals in Munich

(often putting in a twelve-hour day) for their forthcoming tour, for which they'd acquired a new keyboard player – former Boomtown Rat Spike Edney. It took them a while to get into gear, as Taylor explained: "It's strange how rusty we are, and so we're trying to blow the cobwebs away. It's taking a lot of work. Usually we rehearse until about nine, and then we eat together and decide what we're going to do in the evening. The clubs here are really fun. Something to cater for every taste or perversion.

"We still have the rock'n' roll gypsy mentality. Even after twelve years without a line-up change we still really enjoy the buzz from playing live and the fact that we have hit singles. Some bands in our position might take it all in their stride, but we're still like kids – we get very excited."

'Hammer To Fall' was released as a single at the start of September ("a very good pop song," said *Melody Maker*), as was the video of the Montreal concert film *We Will Rock You*; plagued by disaster as a cinema film (plans to show it on a giant screen kept backfiring when the screen kept collapsing), the film was a hit on video, entering the charts at number one. Queen toured Europe until the end of September, then headed off for pastures new. They still had a yen for playing exotic and unexplored (in rock terms) places, and had even looked into the possibility of playing a gig in the Vatican (but the Pope said no), as Taylor explained: "The Russians still think we're very decadent. We want to play China as well, and Korea. John and I spent a holiday in Korea, and it's a fascinating place." But now they'd agreed to play twelve shows in South Africa's notorious Sun City – a gambling resort for the idle rich which had been blackballed by the United Nations because of South Africa's policy of apartheid.

From the start, the group were aware that their decision to play Sun City was a controversial one, and attempted to explain themselves in advance. "We've thought about the morals of it a lot, and it's something we've decided to do," said May. "This band is not political, we play to anybody who comes to listen. The show will be in Bophuthatswana in front of a mixed audience."

Deacon echoed his sentiments: "Throughout our career we've been a very

non-political group. We enjoy going to new places. We've toured America and Europe so many times that it's nice to go somewhere different. Everybody's been to South Africa – it's not as though we're setting a precedent. Elton John's been there, Rod Stewart, Cliff Richard... I know there can be a bit of a fuss, but apparently we're very popular down there... Basically, we want to play wherever the fans want to see us."

And Taylor took a more aggressive stance : "'I Want To Break Free' is an unofficial anthem among the African Congress movement, and 'Another One Bites the Dust' is one of the biggest selling songs in South African black history."

Queen flew to Bophuthatswana at the start of October, and on October 5 played their first concert at the Sun City Superbowl... but fifteen minutes into the show Freddie's voice gave out. They finished the concert, but Mercury was in a lot of pain. Specialists confirmed that it was a recurrence of his old throat problem, aggravated by the dry South African air. Complete rest was ordered, and the next five shows were cancelled. Brian May was restless from the enforced inactivity and wanted to see more of South Africa than the sheltered confines of Sun City; when he was asked to present prizes at the annual 'Black African Awards' show in Soweto, he accepted. He found the experience a moving one: "It was amazing. The whole atmosphere, the warmth, the great friendliness of the people – you could feel it, it was almost a tangible thing. It was a night I will never forget. I promised those people that one day Queen would go back to Soweto and play the stadium for them."

Freddie's voice recovered, and the final six shows went without a hitch. As a parting gift, Queen decided to donate all royalties from a special live album to a school for blind and deaf children in Bophuthatswana.

Returning home, Queen faced some unexpected repercussions of their visit when they discovered that they'd broken a Musician's Union ruling by playing in South Africa. May defended their actions before a meeting of the Union's general committee: "I told them we believed that we achieved more in the fight against apartheid by going, and insisting on mixed audiences, than by staying away; that

we had been able and willing to have our anti-apartheid views printed in the South African press (unusual at that time), that we had been able to give moral support to many minority groups by being there, and had been praised for our courage in going there by all who were trying to break down the barriers, and that if we were to refuse to play to people suffering under a government we didn't approve of, there would be very few places we could go (maybe not even Britain). Finally, I upheld our belief that music should transcend all barriers, unfettered by race or politics."

May's speech was well received, but his arguments had little effect on the committee, and the group was heavily fined by the Union. Naturally, the rock press also hammered the group for playing South Africa, accusing them of naïveté at best, (implied) racism at worst, and the spectre of Sun City would plague the band for a long time to come. Roger attempted to clear the air: "In a way I do regret playing. In some ways I would defend what we did. I mean, basically we play music to people – lots of them, preferably – and I think a lot of crap is talked over here about things that people don't really know about." Brian May was more emphatic: "We're totally against apartheid and all it stands for, but I feel we did a lot of bridge building. We actually met musicians of both colours. They all welcomed us with open arms. The only criticism we got was from outside South Africa."

Doubtless glad that the year was coming to an end, Queen released a special Christmas single, aptly titled 'Thank God It's Christmas' (it reached number twenty-one). 1984 had been a *very* mixed year. On the one hand, Queen had become almost respectable when they were awarded a Nordoff Robbins Silver Clef award for their "Outstanding Contribution To British Music". However, as a result of playing Sun City, they now also found themselves on the United Nations' cultural blacklist.

QUEEN
A Kind of Magic

A Kind Of Magic

EMI EU 3509

In January 1985, Queen headlined at the 'Rock In Rio' festival in Brazil, playing to 250,000 fans. The first concert was a triumph, but the second came eight days later – and it had rained solidly for those eight days, turning the arena into a swamp (the festival toilet facilities were also less than ideal). Still, it was a memorable gig, and a good one (when the 'Live In Rio' concert video was released later in the year, it topped the video charts). In April they toured New Zealand and Australia, before heading on to Japan in May.

And on April 29 Freddie Mercury finally released his first solo album, 'Mr Bad Guy' (another single, 'I Was Born To Love You' had been released earlier that month). "I've put my heart and soul into this album," he said at the time. "It's much more beat oriented than Queen's music, and it also has some very moving ballads.

"They're all love songs, things to do with sadness and pain. At the same time they're frivolous and tongue in cheek; that's my nature. I've wanted to do a solo album for a long time, and the rest of the band have encouraged me to do it. I wanted to cover such things as reggae rhythms, and I've done a couple of tracks with a symphony orchestra." Possibly living (and partying) in Munich had brought Freddie out of himself more – he'd been seen regularly on the London club scene over the previous year – and in the same interview he seemed more willing to talk candidly about his personal life, love, and the pressures of fame: "I seem to eat people up and destroy them. There must be a destructive element in me, because I try very hard to build up relationships, but somehow I drive people away. They always blame the end of the love affair on me, because I'm the successful one. Whoever I'm with seems to get into a battle of trying to match up to me, and

over-compensating... Then they end up treading all over me!

"I can't win. Love is Russian Roulette for me. No one loves the real me inside, they're all in love with my fame, my stardom. I fall in love far too quickly and end up getting hurt all the time. I've got scars all over. But I can't help myself because basically I'm a softie – I have this hard, macho shell which I project on stage, but there's a much softer side too, which melts like butter.

"I try to hold back when I'm attracted to someone, but I just can't control love. It runs riot. All my one-night stands are just me playing my part. What I really like is a lot of loving. And I spoil my lovers terribly, I like to make them happy and I get so much pleasure out of giving them really wonderful, expensive presents... You can have everything in the world and still be the loneliest man, and that is the most bitter type of loneliness." Asked about his rumoured bisexuality, he replied, "I couldn't fall in love with a man the way I could with a girl."

He also talked about his wealth: "I love having so much money, but I don't believe in counting it. And because I have far more than I need, I give a lot of it away to people that I like. I try to enjoy life, and if there was no money I wouldn't let it stop me having a good time. In the early days, when I had hardly anything, I'd save for two weeks and then blow it all in a day so that I could have a blast of fun."

And about his feelings for his ex-lover, Mary Austin. Their physical relationship had ended some time before (and by this point, Freddie's companions were reportedly usually male), but he had bought her a flat near his house, and she also worked for him, managing his domestic staff and business affairs: "Our love affair ended in tears, but a deep bond grew out of it, and that's something nobody can take away from us. It's unreachable. All my lovers ask me why they can't replace her, but it's simply impossible.

"I don't feel jealous of her lovers because, of course, she has a life to lead, and so do I. Basically, I try to make sure she's happy with whoever she's with, and she tries to do the same for me. We look after each other, and that's a wonderful form of love. I might have all the problems in the world, but I have Mary and that gets me through. What better person to

leave my fortune to when I go? Of course, my parents are in my will, and so are my cats, but the vast bulk of it will go to Mary.

"If I dropped dead tomorrow, Mary's the one person I know who could cope with my vast wealth. She works in my organisation and looks after my money side and all my possessions. She's in charge of the chauffeurs, maids, gardeners, accountants and lawyers. All I have to do is throw my carcass around on stage!"

Soon he would throw it about on the most memorable occasion of his career. In December 1984, moved by the plight of those starving in Ethiopia, Bob Geldof had assembled an all-star cast (under the banner of Band Aid) for a benefit single, 'Do They Know It's Christmas'. It became the UK's biggest-selling single ever, and the inevitable question of a follow-up was raised. Rather than make another record, Geldof decided to organise a concert – with the biggest rock names he could get – taking place simultaneously at London's Wembley Stadium and in Philadelphia. To raise even more money for Ethiopia, the event would be televised live around the globe... and if there was one group whose popularity in South America (and other non-Western territories) was beyond doubt, that group was Queen. Geldof desperately wanted them on board, to convince those countries' TV stations to take part in the satellite link-up.

Queen were initially approached by Spike Edney, Geldof's pal from The Boomtown Rats, who was playing keyboards for them at the time. As May later recalled, the group were initially dubious about the whole thing: "Actually, it's only by a narrow squeak that we got involved in it. Our first reaction was, 'Oh, God – not another one!' We'd been involved in quite a few, and we were a bit disillusioned as to how the whole business works."

Geldof then met with Jim Beach to assuage Queen's fears that a short set (each band was to be allowed only twenty minutes) would only cause tension and problems on the day. As John Deacon later recalled: "We didn't know Bob Geldof at all. When 'Do They Know It's Christmas' was out, that was a lot of the newer acts. For the gig, he wanted to get a lot of the established acts. Our first reaction was, we didn't know – twenty minutes, no soundcheck... !

"When it became apparent that it *was* going to happen, we'd actually just finished touring Japan, and ended up having a meal in the hotel discussing whether we should do it, because obviously they wanted an answer. And we said yes. We didn't get involved in the running order thing, but strangely enough we did well coming on when we did... "

Queen rehearsed intensely for three days before the event, and then took to the stage at Wembley Stadium on July 13. They came on at six p.m., and were the first group to be seen in the States, since the satellite link-up to Philadelphia kicked in at the same time. And, as most observers later agreed, with the possible exception of U2 they virtually stole the show. Few other bands could have crammed *quite* as many hit singles into a twenty minute set as smoothly as Queen did and – as an acerbic Bob Geldof later commented, "Freddie was in his element – being able to ponce around with the whole world watching."

As a result of their appearance on Live Aid, Queen's record sales *soared*, and while this was true for virtually every act who played Live Aid (except Adam Ant, whose sales apparently went down), it was *particularly* true for Queen. It seemed that thousands of people had realised overnight that they actually liked Queen after all. The event superseded Woodstock in the public imagination (and the history books) as the gig of the century, raised £50 million for charity, and hopefully saved a few lives as well.

John Deacon summed up Queen's feelings about the event: "It was the one day that I was proud to be involved in the music business – a lot of days you certainly don't feel that! But that day was fabulous – people there forgot that element of competitiveness... It was a good morale booster for us too, because it showed us the strength of support we had in England, and it showed us what we had to offer as a band."

In August Freddie was seen in public with a new companion, 42-year-old German actress Barbara Valentin. "Barbara and I have formed a bond which is stronger than anything I've had with a lover for the last six years," Mercury said. "I can really talk to her and be myself in a way that's very rare." Mercury also threw a lavish party for his 39th birthday the following month, with all the guests (male and

QUEEN

female) coming in drag (except Freddie). He had the whole thing filmed for use in the promotional video for his next solo single, 'Living On My Own', but the record company deemed the video a bit too hot to handle (though attitudes to transvestism must have changed since then; the single was remixed in 1993, and subsequently charted – and the video was being shown on Saturday morning TV!).

But Live Aid did more than just revive the group's public profile. The experience inspired them to write 'One Vision', released in November (it was the first time in the band's career that all four members had collaborated on a single). The video featured a nice touch – it kicked off with Queen's faces in the same set-up as for the 'Bohemian Rhapsody' video ten years earlier.

The press release for 'One Vision' stated simply that the song had been "inspired" by Live Aid (though it had also apparently been inspired by the "I have a dream" speech of Martin Luther King). Queen were consequently accused in some quarters of attempting to cash in on the event (which was practically akin to blasphemy; Geldof was well on the way to his halo by this point). Roger Taylor remarked, "I was absolutely devastated when I saw that in the press. It was a terrible mistake and I was really annoyed about it. Some public relations person got hold of the wrong end of the stick. I went absolutely bananas when I saw that."

May was more pragmatic: "We do a lot of stuff for charities. But 'One Vision' was a way of getting back to what we're doing, and if we didn't run ourselves as a business, we wouldn't be around for the next Live Aid. We're not in the full-time business of charity at all. We're in the business of making music, which is a good enough end in itself." And Queen had donated the song 'Is This The World We Created?' to the Save The Children Fund.

The group had kept active throughout the rest of the year. Taylor had produced a single for actor-turned-singer Jimmy Nail (a cover of 'Love Don't Live Here Anymore'), and been one of several 'guest' drummers who played on Roger Daltrey's tribute to the late Keith Moon, 'Under A Raging Moon'. He'd also played drums and synth on two singles –

Feargal Sharkey's 'Loving You' and Camy Todorow's 'Bursting at The Seams' – both of which he also co-produced, and produced an album for Jason Bonham's new band, Virginia Wolf. Taylor and Deacon also played some sessions with Elton John. Brian May had confined himself to contributing a chapter on electric guitar playing to *The Guitar Teacher's Handbook*, published by Oxford University Press.

They'd begun recording the next album in September, much to John Deacon's relief, as he told an interviewer in November: "We're not so much a *group* anymore. We're four individuals that work together as Queen, but our working together as Queen is actually taking up less and less of our time. I mean, basically I went spare, really, because we were doing so *little*. I got really bored, and I actually got quite depressed."

In November, Freddie took part in Fashion Aid at the Royal Albert Hall – the fashion industry's fund-raising event for Ethiopia. Freddie wore a suit made by Her Dianaship's favourite designers, the Emmanuels, accompanying actress Jane Seymour (in an Emmanuels wedding dress) up the catwalk. How camp can you get?

On December 5 a boxed set, 'The Complete Works', was released. This was a limited edition set which included all Queen's albums to date (excluding 'Greatest Hits', but with an extra album – 'Complete Vision' – which rounded up all the stray singles and B-sides, up to and including 'One Vision'). All the albums had been digitally re-mastered, and the package included two booklets and a map showing Queen's worldwide conquests.

But one country in particular was still causing them trouble. At the beginning of December Steve Van Zandt's Artists Against Apartheid released the 'Sun City' single and album, which condemned the resort and all those who played there. The song got plenty of radio airplay, and Sun City became the subject of a great deal of media discussion. In this climate, no band in their right mind would have *dreamt* of playing there... nevertheless, Sun City's entertainment director Hazel Feldman told *NME* that "a return appearance by Queen should not be ruled out." On December 14, Queen issued the following rebuttal: "Queen categorically state that they have no plans, at

present, to return to Sun City and wish to make it plain that they have a total abhorrence of apartheid."

1985 had also sounded another dark note: one of Freddie's friends, 35-year-old courier Tony Bastin had died of AIDS. He would not be the last.

January 1986 saw Queen in the studio, busily working on their new album. They'd been approached by film director Russell Mulcahy (a veteran of pop video) to provide a theme tune for Mulcahy's feature film début, a $20 million fantasy epic called *Highlander*. After seeing a rough edit of the film, Queen got enthusiastic enough to provide the entire film soundtrack.

Freddie also found time to record a song titled 'Hold On' (a duet with his friend Jo Dare) for the soundtrack of a German film, *Zabou* as well as guesting on Billy Squier's 'Enough Is Enough' album. Meanwhile, Roger produced an album for Birmingham band Magnum; John co-wrote a song for Errol Brown's solo album.

In March 1986, Queen released the first fruit of the 'Highlander' project, a single, 'A Kind Of Magic', that reached number three in the UK and number one in thirty-five other countries. It was also the title track of the album that was released two months later, in May. The bulk of the album consisted of songs from the movie soundtrack, for which Russell Mulcahy had specifically chosen Queen: "When I did this film, there was only one band in my mind to do the music, and that's Queen. Queen's music was just right for this film – they have a very keen sense of visuals. They write very powerful, anthem-type songs, and the film needed just that kind of energy. I've always been a fan of Queen's and for a long time have wanted to work with them." Queen didn't let Mulcahy down, providing three anthems here that are classics of the genre: 'A Kind Of Magic', 'Friends Will Be Friends' and 'Who Wants To Live Forever?' – the latter being so heavily gizmo-laden that one wondered whether Brian May had brought his kitchen sink into the studio.

Mulcahy also directed the video for the 'A Kind Of Magic' single ("It's a kind of magic," is a line of dialogue from the film's hero; but whether the song or the dialogue came first is unknown), filmed at the old BBC Playhouse. "It will please the six to sixty-year-olds,"

Mulcahy said of the video, "with magic and fantasy like we used to see in the old musicals of Hollywood." Much the same could be said for *Highlander* itself, an enjoyable romp which united the screen's best Tarzan (Christopher Lambert) and best James Bond (Sean Connery) for an epic sword and sorcery tale of love and revenge across four centuries. "There's some very heavy stuff in the film," said Taylor. "It's a very heavy film." Mulcahy also made another video, for the US single 'Princes of The Universe', starring Christopher Lambert in his *Highlander* role. *Highlander* itself received its UK première at the Queen fan convention in April. The album entered the UK chart at number one but, as usual, provoked attacks from the critics: "Queen have been plying their trade profitably for so long now that there's really no point in becoming incensed at their one (lack of) vision. The only strong emotion Queen now evoke in me is a fervent wish that Brian May would cut his hair," said *Record Mirror*.

That same month John Deacon released his first solo single, 'No Turning Back', taken from yet another movie soundtrack – that of Biggles, (loosely) based on the exploits of W.E. Johns' fictional flying ace. And Freddie Mercury also released a solo single, of the title theme from his old friend Dave Clark's new rock musical *Time*, which reached 24 on the charts. Like fellow soundtrack contributor Stevie Wonder, Mercury had declined to take part in the lavish stage production of *Time* that Clark – formerly of The Dave Clark Five – staged in London. But he did turn up to see it, and spent the intermission disguised as an ice cream vendor, throwing free ice cream into the audience. At first he was going to actually sell the stuff, but as his friend Joe Fanelli pointed out, he wouldn't have a clue what a pound coin looked like, so how could he give people change?

On May 29 Roger and Dominique had their second child, a daughter named Rory. But it was Brian May who grabbed the tabloids' attention that month, when his name became romantically linked with Anita Dobson, star of the BBC TV soap opera *EastEnders*.

QUEEN
LIVE MAGIC

Live Magic

EMI EMC 3519

For an eight-week period (from June until August 1986), Queen toured solidly through Scandinavia, Germany, France, Belgium, Switzerland, Spain, Eire and the UK. But – post Live Aid – Queen were now bigger than ever. Ticket applications for their two shows at Wembley Stadium in July numbered close to half a million, and tickets for the Newcastle concert sold out within an hour of going on sale. Announcing that Queen would play an extra open-air show at Knebworth Park in August, promoter Harvey Goldsmith stated at a press conference that, "The queue of ticket applicants at Newcastle was longer than the queue for Cup Final tickets when Newcastle United were in the FA Cup Final. The Manchester show was the fastest selling show ever to be advertised in that city. I've never known anything like it. We were overwhelmed at the demand for Wembley Stadium tickets, but not surprised. However, the rush for the Newcastle and Manchester shows went beyond our wildest dreams. I'm really thrilled. It just shows that after fifteen years Queen are bigger than ever."

The new concerts introduced a new stage show, based around a 160 foot stage – big enough to fill one end of Wembley Stadium, and requiring holes to be drilled in the Stadium's concrete foundations – and utilising a new Clare Brothers sound system and the largest lighting rig ever assembled. The general effect, according to Roger, would be "bigger than bigness itself. It'll make *Ben-Hur* look like the Muppets."

The band rehearsed solidly for four weeks before the tour kicked off – "more than we have ever done in our career," admitted Taylor, who added, "I think we are probably the best live band in the world at the moment, and we are going to prove it – no one who comes to see us will be disappointed."

At the end of the first gig, in Stockholm,

Freddie unveiled his latest outfit for curtain calls: yards of red velvet cloak (trimmed with ermine) draped around him, and a gold crown on his head. It became a crowd pleaser everywhere they played.

'Friends Will Be Friends' was released as a single in June to coincide with the tour (it reached number 14 on the charts) ; three months later, 'Who Wants To Live Forever' was released (and reached number 24). In July Freddie also released a video EP featuring four tracks : 'I Was Born To Love You', 'Made In Heaven', 'Time' and 'Living On My Own'. The last track having been banned from TV broadcast, the EP became an instant collector's item.

In July the tour reached Britain (it was sponsored by Harp Lager in the UK), and all profits from the Newcastle show were donated to the Save The Children Fund. Queen aide Jim Beach commented, "Queen were so bowled over at the amount of enthusiasm for their shows they wanted to say 'thank you'. Princess Anne's dedication to Save The Children goes beyond the call of duty and is an example to us all." After the second of their two nights at Wembley (which was filmed by Tyne Tees TV), Queen threw a celebratory party at the Roof Garden which featured nude waitresses, drag artists – and Queen playing a short set with guest vocalists Fish (from Marillion, who'd been supporting Queen on tour), Samantha Fox and Gary Glitter.

After the UK dates they returned to Europe, and later that month played to 80,000 fans in Budapest's Nepstadium. They were the first Western musical act to appear in Hungary since Louis Armstrong played there in 1964. The stage was transported to Hungary by road (in sections, on fifteen lorries), and after it had arrived it took the 60-strong road crew two days to assemble it. Five generators and eight miles of cabling were needed to power the sound and the light rig (which included two PA towers, complete with searchlights). Queen themselves travelled to Hungary in style – from Vienna (their last gig), they sped by hydrofoil down the Danube (the hydrofoil belonged to USSR President Mikhail Gorbachev).

Amazingly, the audience – who had come not just from Hungary, but from all over the Eastern Bloc countries – sang along as avidly

QUEEN

as their Western counterparts, and knew all the words to 'Love Of My Life'. In return, the group performed a traditional Hungarian folk song, 'Tavaski Szel', and when Freddie appeared draped in a Union Jack he quickly flipped it over to reveal the Hungarian flag embroidered on the reverse. Naturally, the audience went nuts. A video of the show was released in February 1987 (filmed by the government-owned Hungarian company Mafilm).

Staying in a ritzy Budapest hotel, Freddie managed to collar the Presidential Suite for himself. Taylor commented on the mind-boggling dimensions of Freddie's suite, to which Freddie supposedly replied, "All suites are equal, my dear... but some are more equal than others." To which Taylor allegedly responded, "Well, it's a fuck sight more equal than mine!"

Two weeks later, they were back in Britain, playing to an audience of 150,000 at Knebworth Park in Hertfordshire. The equipment statistics were getting increasingly staggering: for Knebworth Queen used a six thousand square foot stage, 180 Clare Brothers S4 speaker cabinets, 8.6 miles of cable, five power generators producing 5,000 amps, plus an immense sound system (half a million watts) that included special delay towers to take account of the venue's size. In addition, instead of the usual arrangement of video screens either side of the stage, Queen chose instead to mount one huge (20 foot by 30 foot) Starvision screen over the centre of the stage. The 25-ton screen was on top of a tower; to anchor this securely required laying foundations of concrete, and the counterbalance of a huge water reservoir at the back of the stage (plus 25 skips full of sand used as ballast).

Knebworth was a triumphant show, marred only by a small outbreak of crowd violence, and the stabbing of a fan close to the stage (on the plus side, a baby was born in the crowd). At the end, Freddie saluted the crowd as usual, wrapped in ermine and holding a fur-trimmed crown aloft in his right hand. Little did anybody realise that this would be his last appearance with Queen on a concert stage.

Freddie finally moved into his Kensington mansion, six years after buying it (during which time it had been completely refurbished, and

practically rebuilt). He'd also bought the two mews cottages next door, so as to enlarge the house even more. Here Mercury would happily live out his remaining years, with his assistants Feebie and Joe, his companion Jim Hutton, and a small litter of cats.

In November the Tyne Tees film of Queen's Wembley show was broadcast on Channel 4, with simulcast stereo on the nation's independent radio stations. It picked up a viewing audience of 3.5 million.

Brian May produced an album – 'Cancelled' – for Japanese singer Minako Honda, and fended off rumours about his relationship with Anita Dobson. The duo consistently denied they were anything more than friends, as Brian was concerned about protecting his children from the tabloid jackals.

In December Queen issued a great souvenir from a great tour – the 'Live Magic' album. Though it didn't even get released in the USA ("Queen couldn't get arrested in the States right now," said May bitterly. Their relationship with Capitol had definitely not worked out well), in the UK – even without a single release for radio stations to latch onto – the album shifted over 400,000 copies by Christmas, and reached number three.

And deservedly so. Queen's second live LP is *miles* better than their first. Recorded at three concerts on the 1986 Magic Tour (Wembley, Knebworth and Budapest), the album managed to deliver decent sound and solid performances – even including a creditable (given the absence of David Bowie) version of 'Under Pressure'. Some critics found the track selection curious, as several of the group's biggest hits were notable by their absence, and objected to the fact that these were edited highlights, rather than one complete concert (but if they preferred 'Live Killers', they must be deaf). But it's a fun album – by now, Queen had stadium rock down to a fine art, and the crowd dutifully sang along almost constantly (even when Freddie did his scales), aural proof that a Queen concert was a real *event*. Freddie may not have achieved his dream of bringing ballet to the masses, but he took his audience to the last night of The Proms, and they loved him for it.

QUEEN
THE MIRACLE

PARLOPHONE PCSD 107

Queen had decided that 1987 would be another year off – they needed the rest. Deacon and Taylor spent the first few months of the year holidaying in LA, while May attempted to sort out his tangled personal life. His wife Chrissy gave birth to their second daughter Emily Ruth in February, but Brian was by now deeply involved with Anita Dobson. Freddie alone was concentrating on work, recording some solo material at Townhouse Studios. The first fruit of this – a cover version of The Platters' classic 'The Great Pretender' – was released at the end of February, and reached number four on the UK chart. The video for the song featured Freddie, Peter Straker and Roger Taylor all dressed in drag.

When the announcements of the nominees for that year's BPI Awards were made, Queen didn't even get a mention. In retaliation EMI took out an ad in the event's official programme (and the music trade press) listing Queen's achievements during 1986. It read as follows :

1) Queen sold 1,774,991 albums in the UK alone.

2) 'A Kind Of Magic' entered the UK album chart at number one and remained in the Top Five for thirteen consecutive weeks.

3) The 1,828,375th fan in the UK bought a copy of 'Queen's Greatest Hits', and the album continued in the UK Top 100 charts throughout the year, where it has been for 268 weeks.

4) Queen sold out two nights at Wembley Stadium, one night at Newcastle St James's Park, one night at Manchester Maine Road and one night at Knebworth – total in excess of 400,000 people – an all-time UK attendance record.

5) Queen's 'Real Magic', directed by Gavin Taylor, became the first ever stereo simulcast on independent television and the independent radio network when a satellite link-up took place on 25 October.

6) Queen's 657th performance became the first

ever major stadium concert in the Eastern bloc on 27 July at the Nepstadium in Budapest, filmed with 17 35mm movie cameras by the Hungarian State Film Agency, Mafilm.

7) Queen's 'Magic In Budapest', directed by Janos Zsombolyai, became the first full-length feature concert film to be premièred in the Eastern bloc in Budapest's National Congress Hall on 12 December.

8) Queen released their first ever video single in the UK, entering the video charts at number one on 27 October.

9) Queen's Magic Tour of Europe played to over 1 million people in June, July and August in twenty-six dates, grossing in excess of £11 million pounds.

10) *Daily Mirror* readers voted Queen the 'best band' of 1986 by 50 per cent more votes than any other band.

11) *Daily Mirror* readers voted Freddie Mercury 'Best Male Vocalist' for 1986 'by miles'.

12) Freddie Mercury's video EP entered the UK video chart at number one on 21 July.

13) Queen held their first ever three-day fan club convention at Great Yarmouth on 25 April.

14) Russell Mulcahy's second feature film, *Highlander*, with a music score by Queen and Michael Kamen went on general release in the UK on 29 August.

15) Queen threw 28 parties.

16) Queen gave their proceeds of their Newcastle Football Ground concert to the Save The Children Fund.

17) Richard Gray spent 918 hours working on Queen artwork and received 'best album cover' award from the *Daily Express*.

18) Queen released 'Live Magic' on 1 December and sold over 400,000 before Christmas without a single.

19) Queen hits were released on no fewer than fifty-three compilation albums in twenty-three countries throughout the world.

20) Freddie Mercury was forty.

21) Queen refused to ban their videos from appearing on British television.

22) Queen Films had five videos in the UK Top Twenty-five on 8 November.

23) Freddie Mercury was voted 'best male vocalist' of the year by the readers of *The Sun*.

24) Queen were voted 'best group' of the year by Capital Radio listeners.

25) Mary Turner described Queen as a national institution.

26) Queen's 'We Will Rock You' re-entered the

Music Week Top Ten video charts in July, where it remained for the rest of the year.

27) Queen's 'Greatest Flix' remained in the *Music Week* Top Thirty video charts all year totalling 115 consecutive weeks since being the first ever number one video in the UK.

28) Queen's 'Live In Rio' remained in the *Music Week* Top Thirty video charts all year, totalling eighty consecutive weeks since its début at number one on 20 May 1985.

29) Queen were awarded 'top music video' for 'Live In Rio' at the British Video Awards on 16 October.

30) Shell adopted 'I Want To Break Free' as their main theme song for a nation-wide television and radio campaign.

31) Hannes Rossacher and Rudi Dolezal nearly finished post-production on their mammoth video cassette 'Queen - Magic Years (A Visual Anthology)' – due for release early 1987.

32) Yet again Queen fail to win a BPI Award.

Thank you Brian, John, Freddie and Roger - we at EMI appreciate you.

Heavy sarcasm, or what? The BPI would *eventually* honour Queen with an award, but it took them a few more years. Maybe the ad didn't help...

At the end of May, at Ibiza's chic Ku Club, Freddie unveiled his latest extra-curricular outing: a collaboration with operatic diva Montserrat Caballe. "I just think she has a remarkable voice... I happened to mention it on Spanish TV and she called me up," said Freddie, a long-time fan of Caballe's who'd written 'Barcelona' at her request to celebrate the joys of her native city, now chosen to host the forthcoming 1992 Olympics. They premièred the song as part of an Olympics celebration party, which featured the largest fireworks display ever staged in Europe. "It's like a dream come true, working with her," Freddie told one reporter, admitting his hopes of their recording a whole album together.

They'd actually begun work on an album that April, but it took nine months to complete, since Caballe's availability was limited. Freddie and his co-writer Mike Moran had to complete tracks in their entirety, so that Caballe could just come in and add her vocal (usually completed in one take). Mercury was ecstatically pleased with the results; when the album was completed

he was heard to ask, "What else is there left for me to do?" Well, he *did* finally shave that moustache off as well. Released in October as a single, 'Barcelona' reached number eight.

May meanwhile had earlier in the year recorded one track with heavyweight rocker Meatloaf, 'A Time For Heroes', which became the theme for LA's sporting event for the handicapped, the Paralympic Games. He also produced the début album from Bad News – like Spinal Tap, a parody heavy metal band (not that heavy metal really *needs* parodying) comprised of Comic Strip players Rik Mayall, Ade Edmondson, Nigel Planer and Peter Richardson. As May recounted, "I think we made a great album, but unfortunately it's not the kind of thing that can get commercial success as it's directed at a minority audience. But I think it's a very astute comment on rock music and the way that it's moved over the last few years. It was recorded live and mainly unscripted. They didn't use their real names and we addressed each other in character. They weren't pretending they were rock stars – they *were* rock stars." Amazingly, the Bad News version of 'Bohemian Rhapsody' managed to reach number 44 in the UK charts. Anita Dobson's single 'Talking Of Love' (produced by Brian) was released in July, and the pair flew to Vienna to shoot the video for the song. Even on a *Wogan* appearance, they still denied they were romantically involved.

Roger Taylor was also restless and seeking activity, as he said that summer: "Queen is like a huge rolling machine and we're not working all the time. I am a musician by profession – that's my whole life. I don't want to waste it... " Taylor's way out of inactivity was a practical one: with the blessings of the others (and on the understanding that Queen would always come first) he placed a small ad in *Melody Maker*, and subsequently (July) auditioned 250 musicians in London with a view to forming a working band. The final line-up for his new group, The Cross, were Taylor on lead vocals and rhythm guitar, Spike Edney on keyboards, Josh Macrae on drums, Peter Noone (no relation to Herman the Hermit) on bass and Clayton Moss on lead guitar. "I wanted to be in a working group," Taylor explained. "I want to play music I sincerely believe in, that was heavy rock 'n' roll, and I want to do it live. The solo LPs were my own expression of my own musical product at the time. This is a whole new group which is going to be taken seriously, I hope – this is a whole new career."

Taylor took The Cross off for rehearsals in Ibiza – where, a couple of months later, Freddie celebrated his 41st birthday in style, flying in all his friends from London on a private plane. The Cross then flew off to record their début album, in Montreux and London. Their first Cross single 'Cowboys And Indians' was released on Virgin in September, but failed to set the world alight. Taylor did at least gain one positive result from the experience – he met Debbie Leng, the ex-Cadbury's Flake model, who'd taken a part as an extra in The Cross's video. The pair were soon romantically involved.

Meanwhile, Freddie discussed AIDS frankly in an interview he gave in late 1987: "I lived for sex. Amazingly, I've just gone completely the other way. AIDS changed my life – I have stopped going out, I've become almost a nun. I was extremely promiscuous, but I've stopped all that. What's more, I don't miss that kind of life.

"Anyone who has been promiscuous should have a test," he concluded. He'd already had one, he confirmed, but it had been negative: "I'm fine, I'm clear."

November saw the release of an interesting three-hour-long video documentary, 'Queen – The Magic Years: A Visual Anthology', produced by Rudi Dolezal and Hannes Rossacher. The duo had taken a couple of years to compile the film, using archive footage and film they'd shot especially.

In January 1988 The Cross released their début album, 'Shove It' (featuring contributions from both Freddie and Brian), and then set off on a low-key tour of the college circuit. Taylor must have felt a distinct sense of déjà vu. Perhaps he was reliving his youth...

Or perhaps he just wanted to get away from the press. In January he'd also married his long-time girlfriend Dominique (Freddie and Mary Austin were the witnesses at the wedding), by whom he had two children. But this wedding was done solely to protect his children's legal status; less than a month later, Roger moved out of the house he shared with his family, and into another home with Debbie Leng. The tabloids, inevitably, found plenty to say about the ageing rocker and his 25-year-old Flake girl.

Brian May was also under tabloid scrutiny, poor sod. In June his father died, and he passed through a period of deep depression; shortly afterwards he made the painful decision to finally

leave his wife, and moved in with Anita Dobson. The media made a meal of it, predictably enough. One of the few moments of joy May can have had in this period came four days after his father's death, when he and John Deacon appeared as part of an all-star pick-up band (alongside Phil Collins, Eric Clapton, Mark Knopfler, Joe Cocker and Elton John) at a concert for the Prince's Trust: "A highlight for me was working with Joe Cocker. His presence seemed to infuse the 'scratch-band' with an amazing energy. And I was able to play alongside Clapton in 'A Little Help From My Friends'. A thrill !"

In April, Freddie Mercury appeared on stage for one performance of *Time*, a benefit show in aid of the AIDS charity the Terrence Higgins Trust. And in October he made a triumphant entry into Barcelona, joining Montserrat Caballe in an all-star gala concert to celebrate the city's successful bid to host the 1992 Olympics. Support acts included Eddy Grant, Spandau Ballet, Jerry Lee Lewis and Rudolf Nureyev... but the highlight came when Freddie (resplendent in tuxedo) and La Caballe (backed by the Barcelona Opera House Orchestra and choir) closed the show with 'Barcelona'. An absence of microphones indicates they were (obviously) miming, as Freddie later explained: "We'd need a lot of rehearsals... they're complex songs and we just didn't have enough time." All proceeds from the event were donated to the International Red Cross.

The duo's operatic album, also titled 'Barcelona' was released later that month and reached number 25. "I don't know how Queen fans will react to this," Mercury said just before the album's release. "The worst thing they can call it is rock opera, which is so *boring* actually. You can't label it in any way because I'm doing songs that I've never done before, the sort of songs to suit our voices. I found it very difficult writing them and singing them because all the registers had to be right and they're all duets." Reviews were mixed, but the rock press liked it more than the straight press did. At least it was different...

November saw the release of the album Brian May had produced for Anita Dobson, 'Talking Of Love'. She had previously (in 1986) reached number four in the charts with a vocal version of the *EastEnders* theme tune, and was more at home belting out show tunes than singing rock. "I think we produced an album that

strides across the two worlds in which we live," May commented. "There's a certain amount of rock influence and a certain amount of show influence. Most of Anita's audience may have thought that it was getting too heavy and most of those in my world thought, 'what the hell's he doing with someone who's really only a show tune singer?'... I stand by the project as being very worthwhile." The previous month – in the midst of (totally fabricated) tabloid speculation that the couple had parted – Dobson released a single from the album, a cover version of The Teddy Bears' 'To Know Him Is To Love Him'. "It's enough if you know I'm with him," said Dobson, attempting to hold the media at bay. "I don't want to talk about it, about him or what he's doing. That's his business. Most of my fans are happy I'm with someone. We have to have something that is ours." May had also agreed to contribute to another project with Dobson – a stage musical with Adam Faith, based on the latter's Seventies TV anti-hero, Budgie.

Queen may have been keeping quiet, but May pretty much buried himself in work, guesting on sessions with Living In A Box, Steve Hackett, Holly Johnson, Black Sabbath, Fuzzbox and Lonnie Donegan (now that's what you call *eclectic*). He also jammed alongside Elton John at a Bon Jovi gig in December, and later that month both he and Deacon joined Roger Taylor and The Cross on stage for the encores when The Cross played at a Christmas party for Queen fan club members at London's Hammersmith Palais.

But though Queen had been publicly quiet for a *second* year, they hadn't been idle. In January they began recording their next album, and had continued (on and off) throughout the year; by Christmas it was nearly done. But 1988 had again brought grim news, when another friend of Freddie's, Nicolai Grishanovitch, died from AIDS. Freddie was rumoured to have taken another AIDS test, which again came up negative.

By the beginning of 1989, Queen had sold over 80 million albums worldwide, and had played concerts in front of audiences totalling over six million people. "We're the Cecil B. De Mille of rock'n'roll," said Freddie, "always wanting to do things bigger and better..."

In April Brian was interviewed about his guest appearance on one track of the new Black Sabbath album 'Headless Cross': "I enjoy doing that, although I'm no session musician... Queen

is and will stay the main thing in my life." He did confirm, however, that he was also (finally) working on a solo project, which would contain "Hard, pure heavy metal, weird acoustic songs and God knows what else. There isn't a direction to the album yet, and I think that's one problem I have to sort out. The solo project is mainly about getting all the stuff I've had in my head onto tape, but I've found that some of the ideas I had in mind for solo work have ended up on the Queen album. I think that the best ideas should really be concentrated towards the group, because it's still the best vehicle I can find.

"It's a real strain doing solo projects, because you are on your own. At the end of the day I am left sitting in a studio with an engineer, saying, 'Is this worth anything or not?' And it's very hard to make those judgements." May's solo album would not appear for another three years.

In the meantime, Queen's sixteenth album, 'The Miracle' was released in May and entered the charts at number one (it had gone platinum on advance sales alone), preceded by the single 'I Want It All' (which entered the charts at number three). For the first time, the songwriting credits (and royalties) were shared equally between all four members. As May explained: "We wanted to record a really democratic album and each one of us would be involved in the songwriting. We created a real band feeling without any ego problems. That's one of the reasons that 'The Miracle' has turned into such a better album than 'A Kind Of Magic', for example."

Well, that's a matter of opinion. The three-year lay-off between albums had resulted in... more of the same, really. Once again, the singles are exceptional, while the rest is decidedly less than awesome. At least 'The Invisible Man' was refreshingly Europop.

For the album's cover, designer Richard Gray had used computer animation techniques to blend headshot photographs of the four Queen members into one combination face. It's a pretty eerie image, and the rumour-mongers were quick to allege that it had been done just to distract attention from Freddie's gaunt features.

The rumours of his ill health were compounded by an interview with DJ Mike Reid, in which Freddie announced that he did not intend to tour with Queen to promote the album live: "I want to change the cycle of album, world tour, album, world tour. Maybe we *will* tour, but it will be for totally different reasons. I've personally had it

with these bombastic lights and staging effects. I don't think a 42-year-old man should be running around in his leotard any more."

At least in the video for the next single 'Breakthru', which showed Queen playing on a moving train, Freddie seemed fit and happy. Released in July, 'Breakthru' reached number seven, and in August the next single, 'Invisible Man', reached number twelve (but the following two singles – 'Scandal' and 'The Miracle' – barely made the top thirty). Roger Taylor commented on Queen's fashionability (or not): "It would be bloody ludicrous if Queen made a record using Acid House techniques. It would be jumping on bandwagons, and we've never been ones for that." Taylor also took the opportunity to dismiss speculation about the state of Freddie's health: "Stupid rumours! Freddie is as healthy as ever on the new album. We had a party at Brian's a few days ago and Freddie didn't exactly give the impression he was on his death bed. We've heard that rumour too, but it's ridiculous."

Roger ended up grabbing headlines himself, as a result of his fortieth birthday party, when a battery of spotlights sweeping the skies above his Surrey home were mistaken for UFO's, causing an Orson Welles 'War Of The Worlds'-type panic.

August saw the release of a 'Rare Live' video compilation – again put together by Austrians Hannes and Rudi, and featuring rare live footage from 1973 onwards.

More archive material surfaced in December with the release of 'Queen At The Beeb' on the Band Of Joy record label. The album consists of a 1973 BBC radio session, featuring seven tracks from the first album, plus 'Ogre Battle' from 'Queen II', and is, according to Malcolm Dome's sleeve notes, "An historic effort that still retains a contemporary resonance... vital, valuable and inexorable." Or to put it another way, rough and ready. The album shows a band that has yet to carve its own niche – they sound like Led Zeppelin indulging in a fairy fantasy on an off day. The album entered the charts (for one week only) at number 67.

But 'The Miracle' had given Queen a shot in the arm, after two years of upheavals and personal woes. Filled with that energy, in December they returned to Mountain Studios in Switzerland, to work on their next album together. Hardly anybody suspected that it would be their last.

INNUENDO

PARLOPHONE PCSD 115

When Queen entered the studio after Christmas 1989, according to their co-producer/engineer Dave Richards: "They were chomping at the bit. They just got into the concert hall where I record them and started whipping each other on." Brian May later commented: "We usually have two or three days just playing, finding sounds, just getting the feel of each other again. We keep the multi-track running, and seem to find that there's little bits that really seem to gel." At the end of the year it was announced that Queen's 'Greatest Hits' was the fourth best-selling album of all time (coming in behind Dire Straits' 'Brothers In Arms' and Michael Jackson's 'Thriller' and 'Bad').

On February 18, 1990, Queen were finally awarded a (special) BPI Award, for their outstanding contribution to British music. All four members of the group attended... but Freddie's drawn appearance only heightened the media speculation about his health (he later issued a statement that he'd never felt better). After the awards ceremony the group threw a 20th anniversary party at Groucho's for four hundred guests (including everybody who had ever worked for them) that went on till the cows came home. Debbie Leng wore a £150,000 platinum and diamond necklace – a present from Roger.

Queen resumed recording in March, the same month in which Roger Taylor released his second album with The Cross (now on EMI/Parlophone), 'Mad, Bad And Dangerous To Know'. In Britain it was largely ignored, but sold reasonably in Germany, where the group toured several times. In July, Roger's father died.

That summer May installed a new 16-track studio in his home: "I've been threatening to have it for a long time, as I just had very simple equipment... it's all simple enough for me to work without too much of a problem. I hate too many buttons!"

In September May also jammed live two nights running with Black Sabbath (on the encores), and guested on two tracks on the début album by D-Rock.

In the USA Queen ended their contract with Capitol (they bought it back), signing the US rights to their entire back catalogue in November to the Disney-owned Hollywood records for a reported £10 million. But the hoped-for Christmas release of the new album was put back, to February 1991.

On November 13 *The Sun* announced: 'It's Official ! Freddie is seriously ill', quoting Brian May as saying: "He's okay and he definitely hasn't got AIDS, but I think his wild rock'n' roll lifestyle has caught up with him.

"Freddie didn't want to do any videos for the next album. And he would prefer not to go out on tour either. I think he just needs a break." Later that month Freddie was photographed leaving the Harley Street surgery of Dr F. Gordon Atkinson looking "gaunt and haggard" (according to *The Sun*). A Queen spokesman commented that Freddie had "worked flat out for four months on the new album. He is just exhausted."

Also in November, the Red and Gold Theatre Company's production of *Macbeth* opened at London's Riverside Studios. Music for the production had been specially composed by Brian May. "I'm very aware that the music could be irritating if not done well, and that a lot of people might feel that rock does not fit in with Shakespeare. But Will Shakespeare was into making direct contact with his audience – the way Queen has always done."

Late that year white rapper Vanilla Ice topped both the US and UK charts with his 'Ice Ice Baby', which sampled the bass riff from 'Under Pressure' (and many of us thought that was the song's one redeeming feature). Brian May's comments were guarded: "I just thought, 'interesting, but nobody will ever buy it because it's crap'. Tums out I was wrong... we don't want to get involved in litigation with other artists ourselves, that doesn't seem very cool... now I think it's quite a good bit of work, in its own way."

In December, 'Queen At Wembley' (the 1986 simulcast show directed by Gavin Taylor) was released on video. That month The Cross once again played the Queen fan convention, jamming with May on stage.

In January, at Mercury's insistence, Queen

QUEEN
INNUENDO

returned to the studio in Montreux to record extra material. Originally, these songs were intended as B-sides, but the sessions went so well that it was decided to use the material as the beginnings of yet another album.

Meanwhile the title track of the new album, 'Innuendo', was released as a single at the end of January 1991, and entered the charts at number one. At six and a half minutes long, it was the longest number one since 'Bohemian Rhapsody' (in the US 'Headlong' was released instead, as Hollywood were convinced that 'Innuendo' would get zero airplay). On first listening I thought the song pompous and inflated – Queen sounded like they were just going through the motions, almost parodying themselves. Even so, the bloody thing grows on you, and now I think it's not half bad, in a kitsch kind of way. May commented: "That was one of the first things that came. It's got this bolero-style rhythm, a very strange track. It's a bit of a risk as a single, but it's different and you either win it all or you lose it all."

The album followed in February, and also entered the charts at number one. It deserved to, if only for 'I'm Going Slightly Mad', 'I Can't Live With You' (both of which display Queen's pop sensibility working at its peak), and the gorgeous 'These Are The Days Of Our Lives', a song which has gained an added poignancy with Freddie's passing (on the minus side, 'Headlong' and 'The Hitman' are *still* hideous). *Q* magazine called it "both endearing and enduring", while Tony Parsons dismissed it in *The Daily Telegraph* as "a cross between Led Zeppelin and Kenneth Williams."

That month, as part of that years' Comic Relief activities, Brian May produced 'The Stonk', a single by comedians Hale and Pace that went to number one.

In March Roger Taylor and his girlfriend Debbie Leng became the parents of a son, Rufus Tiger. The couple made news again in May, when it was reported that an, ahem *private* home video had been stolen from their flat. And they made the news yet again when the gates of their Surrey estate gained a new decoration (to the chagrin of their local council): a pair of garden gnomes that lit up in the dark.

But of Freddie there was little word; the group had closed ranks to protect him. Mary Austin later confirmed that Freddie had been "in a great deal of pain" during the recording of the album. "But he carried on working because that's what

he enjoyed. And working helped him have the courage to face his illness." Mercury must have known his time was limited; hence the insistence that Queen began work on their next album.

But the group could scarcely hide the alteration in Freddie's appearance. He'd reportedly dropped from 12 to nine stone in weight, and in the new publicity photographs he looked thin and ill. In the 'Innuendo' video, special effects obscured his face to the point that one wondered why the group had made a video at all. For 'I'm Going Slightly Mad', filmed at a cost of £20,000 at a studio in Wembley, Freddie appeared alongside a trio of tame penguins, wearing a ton of make-up and an elaborately theatrical wig. But the video still made for uncomfortable viewing: Freddie just looked grotesque – and worse, he looked in pain. A Queen spokesman told reporters, "He's fine. He enjoyed making the video and he's delighted to be back." 'I'm Going Slightly Mad' reached number 22, and the next single, 'Headlong', reached number 14.

In May all four members of Queen spent several weeks in the studio in Switzerland. May then went on a promotional radio tour of the USA, and at one point observed: "The group tends to be the most stable family we've got, although it's hard to see how we've stayed together all this time. Roger is the most extreme in extravagance and the rock 'n' roll lifestyle. Freddie is a mystery, nobody ever quite knows where he's coming from. John, too, the archetypal quiet bass player... but he's the leader on the business side, studies the stock market, understands the deals. And me, I think the others would tell you I'm the most pig-headed member of the band." After the radio tour, May retired to the studio to work on his solo album. But his first solo output (in July) was a jingle for a Ford car commercial, 'Driven By You' (most listeners thought it was just a Queen pastiche). And in October, May acted as musical director for a guitar festival in Seville, playing alongside guitarists Nuno Bettencourt (from Extreme), Joe Walsh, Steve Vai and Joe Satriani.

But solo projects were all that May had to look forward to now - Queen's career had ended. And for Freddie Mercury, it was now just a matter of time.

QUEEN

GREATEST HITS II

LONG PLAY CD

Greatest Hits II

PARLOPHONE PMTV 2

In the late summer of 1991, Freddie's former manager Paul Prenter died of AIDS in Dublin. By this point, Mercury seldom left his beloved 28-room Kensington home. The building was now basically a private clinic, with nurses tending Freddie around the clock. His bedroom was fitted with an oxygen tent, to help ease the breathing difficulties he was suffering as a result of AIDS-induced bronchial pneumonia.

His health failing fast, on Saturday November 23, 1991, Freddie Mercury finally issued a statement to the press: "Following the enormous conjecture in the Press over the last two weeks, I wish to confirm that I have been tested HIV positive and have AIDS. I felt it correct to keep this information private to protect the privacy of those around me. However, the time has now come for my friends and fans around the world to know the truth, and I hope that everyone will join with me, my doctors and all those worldwide in the fight against this terrible disease."

A little over 24 hours after issuing this statement, Freddie Mercury died.

The following day, Dr Gordon Atkinson (Freddie's GP) announced grimly that Freddie had "slipped back a little bit today." Freddie's parents Bommi and Jer came to visit, and made their farewells. Sadly, Mary Austin – who had spent most of the day at Freddie's bedside – had to return home on an errand and missed Freddie's passing by a mere ten minutes. Freddie's close friend Dave Clark was at his bedside when he died, at about 7pm. "The doctor had just left," he said later. "I stayed in there with him and then he fell asleep."

The news was announced at midnight on November 24 by publicist Roxy Meade. The official press statement read: "Freddie Mercury died peacefully this evening at his

home in Kensington, London. His death was the result of bronchial pneumonia, brought on by AIDS."

Those close to him were devastated, probably none more so than Mary Austin, an integral part of Freddie's life for the previous 21 years. "It was so sad," she told reporters. "The suffering I witnessed from Freddie was something I never want to see again. It was awful.

"I will remember Freddie with a lot of love and respect," she added. "He was brave right up until the very end."

Freddie's passing made banner headlines in all the British tabloid press, who for once had to put their homophobia on hold and largely reported his death with sympathy (those papers that went for the scandal angle soon changed tack when they sensed the depth of public sadness at Freddie's demise). No one (except Mary and Jim Hutton) knew exactly how long Freddie had been HIV positive ; he'd been in one steady relationship (with Jim) for the previous seven years, and claimed to have "lived like a nun".

Tributes came from Bowie, John Reid, and a thousand other faces from the past. But none could better the words of the announcement made by the surviving Queen members: "We have lost the greatest and most beloved member of our family. We feel overwhelming grief that he has gone, sadness that he should be cut down at the height of his creativity, but above all great pride in the courageous way that he lived and died. It has been a privilege for us to have shared such magical times. As soon as we are able we would like to celebrate his life in the style to which he was accustomed."

Brian May also wrote (for a Queen Fan Club tribute to Freddie, sent out that Christmas): "As you by now know, Freddie was fighting the terrible AIDS disease for many years, and for much of the time even *we* didn't know. For Freddie, his art and his friends were everything – he poured himself with huge vigour into both. He was determined that no hint of frailty should mar his music, or *our* music, or make life difficult for his friends. By refusing to concede anything to the illness, his amazing strength and courage enabled him to continue at full strength in making albums, videos, etc., even though it cost him more and more in private pain. He never in our hearing complained about his lot, and never let despondency creep into his work, his voice seemed to get miraculously better and better. And he died without ever losing control.

"Freddie never wanted sympathy, he wanted exactly what the fans gave him – belief, support and the endorsement of that strangely winding road to excellence that we, Queen, have tried to follow. You gave him support in being the outstandingly free spirit that he was, and is. Freddie, his music, his dazzling creative energy – those are for ever."

The day after Mercury's death, Freddie's staff allowed fans inside the grounds of his Kensington home, to see the enormous carpet of floral tributes laid out beneath a large Christmas tree. That night a deeply moved Elton John introduced on BBC TV a hastily-compiled film tribute to Freddie's life.

Four days after his death, Freddie was cremated at the West London Cemetery in Kensal Green, after a small private service conducted according to the traditions of the Zoroastrian faith. The music of Montserrat Caballe was played, and among those attending (in addition to the surviving members of Queen) were Elton John and Dave Clark. Despite the secrecy with which the funeral arrangements had been made, police were needed to hold back grieving fans. Four hearses were needed just to convey the flowers.

Freddie had asked that money be donated in his name to the AIDS charity the Terrence Higgins Trust, and the surviving members of Queen decided to re-release 'Bohemian Rhapsody' (backed with 'These Are The Days Of Our Lives') with all royalties from sales being donated to the Trust. Queen's mini-opera went straight in at the top of the charts once again, becoming the second biggest selling single of 1991. First time around it had sold 1.3 million; this time, it added an additional 1.1 million sales.

The Terrence Higgins Trust responded warmly to the group's gesture, describing Freddie's death as "a great loss to music". The Trust's chief executive Nick Partridge added, "His death will bring home to millions of music fans and people around the world how AIDS continues to deprive us of so many talented people, so young.

"Freddie Mercury's death reminds us that

HIV, the virus which can lead to AIDS, is a grim fact of life we cannot ignore.

"The Trust is heartened by Queen's decision to donate all record royalties from the re-release of the band's best-known single, 'Bohemian Rhapsody', to the Trust. We also want to thank the friends and fans of Freddie Mercury who have already made donations to help the Trust continue its work." It's reported that Freddie faced the cameras during his final months for an interview designed to help advise and encourage other AIDS sufferers in the future.

Inevitably, Mercury's death meant that Queen product was selling like hot cakes. The 'Greatest Hits II' compilation had been released in October, (at the risk of sounding cynical, the timing couldn't have been better). Taken together with the first 'Hits' album, this 17-track compilation boils off the dregs and leaves you with the cream: an almost seamless procession of casually catchy (i.e. they make it look easy) great pop singles. The album had entered the charts at number one, and by the end of the year it had become the third biggest selling album of the year. And the first 'Greatest Hits' album had by this time become the best selling UK album *ever*. As was inevitable in the wake of Freddie's death, Queen albums sold by the truckload: that December there were no fewer than ten Queen albums in the UK top one hundred. Also, Brian May's first solo single had been released on schedule, on November 25. The week before, realising that Freddie's end was near, May had talked of delaying its release. But a message was relayed back from Freddie's bedside; despite his pain, Mercury was as pragmatic as ever: "Tell him he must release it. What better publicity could you have?" The song reached number six in the charts.

The week after Freddie's death, May and Taylor appeared on early morning TV to talk about Freddie. Visibly drained, they spoke of their loss (and the world's), but added little to what was already known... except to promise that there would be a memorial concert at some point in the future "to celebrate the life of Freddie Mercury."

Two months later, their plans were more concrete. The duo appeared at the British Music Awards ceremony on February 12 to

collect a Brits Award for the best single of 1991 ('Days Of Our Lives'); there was also a special posthumous Award for Freddie. Accepting the awards, Brian said, "I feel a great mixture of emotion. If Freddie were here, he would go and tell me to put this on the mantelpiece. He would say, 'Look, mum, dad – that's what I did and I'm proud'. We're terribly proud of everything Freddie stood for. We feel his spirit is with us." Taylor then came forward to announce that there would be "a concert that would be a tribute to Freddie's life, at Wembley Stadium on April 20."

"AIDS affects us all," he added. "We see the Wembley concert as a tribute to his life, and the fulfilment of his wish to get this message across. I hope you will join us at Wembley." The pair then left the stage, to a standing ovation. Tickets for the benefit concert (it would eventually raise over £10 million for AIDS charities worldwide) went on sale the following day, and sold out within hours despite the fact that no announcements had yet been made as to who was going to be appearing.

At the annual Ivor Novello Awards on April 15, Brian and Roger collected another award for 'Days Of Our Lives' (Best Selling Single), and took the opportunity to present the Terrence Higgins Trust with a 'Bohemian Rhapsody' royalties cheque for over £1 million.

After Queen and their guest stars had rehearsed solidly for nearly a month, and after a special stage had been built for the show (bigger even than that for the 'Magic' tour), on April 20 – Easter Monday – the 72,000 fans in Wembley Stadium (and the millions watching at home) found out just how special the tribute to Freddie was going to be. Many of the fans had slept outside Wembley the night before ; all were given red ribbons to wear, as a symbol of their support for AIDS victims. (Queen had set up a special charity – the Mercury Phoenix Trust – to administer the money raised by the event. The telecast concert had a viewing audience of 6.3 million in the UK, and over a billion worldwide.)

The first half of the show featured various heavy metal acts (Metallica, Extreme, Def Leppard, Guns N' Roses), plus Bob Geldof in a flowery suit, then U2 appeared on video (in a filmed clip of their gig the night before). At half-

time actress Liz Taylor, a veteran AIDS campaigner, came on to urge that the audience start thinking about their future, and use condoms whatever their sexuality. Then came a satellite link-up with Johannesburg, for South African band Mango Grove.

The second half of the show was what the crowd had been waiting for, and the surviving members of Queen didn't disappoint them, performing their greatest hits with a wide variety of guest vocalists and musicians (and performances of widely varying standards, it must be said): Joe Elliott, Tony Iommi, Roger Daltrey, Robert Plant, Paul Young, Seal, Lisa Stansfield, David Bowie and Annie Lennox (performing a stunning 'Under Pressure'), Bowie solo (with Ian Hunter and Mick Ronson), George Michael (who almost stole the show despite Bowie's 'follow *that*' rendition of the Lord's Prayer), Axl Rose and Elton John... Liza Minnelli (and a cast of thousands, but only Liza had a microphone), who closed the show with 'We Are The Champions'. Well, not quite... As Freddie's image flickered on the giant video screen, the Stadium crowd sang 'God Save The Queen' with all their hearts. What else was there to say?

Well, there were a couple of unanswered questions. Would the others continue as Queen without Freddie? To which the answer has to be, probably not. May has since finally released his solo album, but has stated quite categorically that he sees no point in Queen trying to replace Mercury, or in their continuing as a group without him.

But was there any unreleased Queen material in the can, yet to be released? To which the answer is almost certainly 'yes'. In May 1992, Queen released the complete Wembley concert from the 'Magic' tour on a double CD (it entered the charts at number two). There may well be more live material worth hearing, plus there are certainly some studio recordings – the songs Freddie had recorded with Queen in early 1991, and maybe others (two albums' worth, according to some estimates – plus video footage). Doubtless Queen will release some of this material once a suitably respectful distance has passed from the time of Freddie's death. As I write this (August 1993), Freddie is topping the charts yet again, with a remixed version of 'Living On My Own'.

"He was some kind of a man," Marlene

Dietrich said of Orson Welles' character in *Touch Of Evil*, going on to ask "what does it matter what you say about people?" What does it matter what you say about pop groups? If pressed, I'd say that Queen were occasionally pompous, tedious and pretentiously self-indulgent; occasionally revolutionary; more often than not amusing, intelligent and charming... and nearly always idealistic, optimistic and generally positive. I'd say that maybe we should remember them – and him – this way.

Donations to the Terrence Higgins Trust can be made in Freddie Mercury's name. They should be sent to:

The Terrence Higgins Trust,
P.O. Box 40,
London WC1X 8JU

Queen Discography

SINGLES

Keep Yourself Alive/Son And Daughter
EMI 2036 July 1973.

Seven Seas of Rhye/See What A Fool I've Been
EMI 2121 February 1974.

Killer Queen/Flick Of The Wrist
EMI 2229 October 1974.

Now I'm Here/Lily Of The Valley
EMI 2256 January 1975.

Bohemian Rhapsody/I'm In Love With My Car
EMI 2275 October 1975.

You're My Best Friend/39
EMI 2494 July 1976.

Somebody To Love/White Man
EMI 2565 November 1976.

Tie Your Mother Down/You And I
EMI 2593 March 1977.

We Are The Champions/We Will Rock You
EMI 2708 October 1977.

Spread Your Wings/Sheer Heart Attack
EMI 2757 February 1978.

Fat Bottomed Girls/Bicycle Race
EMI 2870 October 1978

Don't Stop Me Now/In Only Seven Days
EMI 2910 January 1979

Love Of My Life (Live)/Now I'm Here (Live)
EMI 2959 June 1979.

Crazy Little Thing Called Love/Spread Your Wings (Live)
EMI 5001 October 1979.

Save Me/Let Me Entertain You (Live)
EMI 5022. January 1980.

Play The Game/A Human Body
EMI 5076 May 1980.

Another One Bites The Dust/Dragon Attack
EMI 5102 August 1980.

Flash/Football Fight
EMI 5126 November 1980.

Body Language/Life Is Real
EMI 5293 April 1982.

Las Palabras De Amour/Cool Cat
EMI 5316 June 1982.

Back Chat/Staying Power
EMI 4325 August 1982.

Radio Ga Ga/I Go Crazy
QUEEN 1 January 1984

I Want To Break Free/Machines (Or Back To Humans)
QUEEN 2 April 1984.

It's A Hard Life/Is This The World We Created?
QUEEN 3 July 1984.

Hammer To Fall/Tear It Up
QUEEN 4 September 1984.

Thank God It's Christmas/Man On The Prowl/Keep Passing Open Windows
QUEEN 5 November 1984.

One Vision/Blurred Vision
QUEEN 6 November 1985.

A Kind Of Magic/A Dozen Red Roses For My Darling
QUEEN 7 March 1986.

Friends Will Be Friends/Seven Seas of Rhye
QUEEN 8 June 1986.

Who Wants To Live Forever/Killer Queen
QUEEN 9 September 1986.

I Want It All/Hang On In There
QUEEN 10 May 1989.

Breakthru'/Stealin'
QUEEN 11 June 1989.

The Invisible Man/Hijack My Heart
QUEEN 12 August 1989.

Scandal/My Life Has Been Saved
QUEEN 14 October 1989.

The Miracle/Stone Cold Crazy
QUEEN 15 November 1989.

Innuendo/Bijou
QUEEN 16 January 1991

I'm Going Slightly Mad/The Hitman
QUEEN 17 March 1991.

Headlong/Mad The Swine
QUEEN 18 May 1991.

The Show Must Go On/Keep Yourself Alive
QUEEN 19 October 1991.

Bohemian Rhapsody/These Are The Days Of Our Lives
QUEEN 20 December 1991.

EPs

Queen's First EP
Good Old Fashioned Lover Boy/Death On Two Legs (Dedicated To ...)/Tenement Funster/White Queen (As It Began)
EMI 2623 June 1977.

ALBUMS

QUEEN
Keep Yourself Alive/Doing All Right/Great King Rat/My Fairy King/Liar/The Night Comes Down/Modern Times Rock N'Roll/Son And Daughter/Jesus/Seven Seas of Rhye
EMI EMC 3006 July 1973.

QUEEN II
Procession/Father To Son/White Queen (As It Began)/Some Day One Day/The Loser/Ogre Battle/The Fairy Fellows Master Stroke/Nevermore/March Of The Black Queen/Funny How Love Is/Seven Seas of Rhye
EMI EMA 767 March 1974.

SHEER HEART ATTACK
Brighton Rock/Killer Queen/Tenement Funster/Flick Of The Wrist/Lily Of The Valley/Now I'm Here/In The Lap Of The Gods/Stone Cold Crazy/Dear Friends/Misfire/Bring Back That Leroy Brown/She Makes Me (Stormtrooper In Stilettoes)/In The Lap Of The Gods ...Revisited
EMI EMC 3061 November 1974.

THE OLD GREY WHISTLE TEST
(One track only: a version of "Keep Yourself Alive" recorded for "The Old Grey Whistle Test" BBC TV programme in September 1973.)
BBC BELP 004 July 1975.

A NIGHT AT THE OPERA
Death On Two Legs (Dedicated To...)/Lazing On A Sunday Afternoon/I'm In Love With My Car/You're My Best Friend/Sweet Lady/Seaside Rendezvous/The Prophets Song/Love Of My Life/Good Company/Bohemian Rhapsody/God Save The Queen
EMI EMTC 103 December 1975.

A DAY AT THE RACES
Tie Your Mother Down/You Take My Breath Away/Long Away/The Millionaire Waltz/You And I/Somebody To Love/White Man/Good Old Fashioned Lover Boy/Drowse/Teo Torriate (Let Us Cling Together)
EMI EMTC 104 December 1976.

NEWS OF THE WORLD
We Will Rock You/We Are The Champions/Sheer Heart Attack/All Dead All Dead/Spread Your Wings/Fight From The Inside/Get Down To Make Love/Sleeping On The Sidewalk/Who Needs You/It's Late/My Melancholy Blues
EMI EMA 784 October 1977.

JAZZ
Mustapha/Fat Bottomed Girls/Jealousy/Bicycle Race/If You Can't Beat Them/Let Me Entertain You/Dead On Time/In Only Seven Days/ Dreamer's Ball/Fun It/Leaving Home Ain't Easy/ Don't Stop Me Now/More Of That Jazz
EMI EMA 788 November 1978.

LIVE KILLERS
We Will Rock You/Let Me Entertain You/ Death On Two Legs (Dedicated To ...)/ Killer Queen /Bicycle Race /I'm In Love With My Car'/Get Down To Make Love/You're My Best Friend/Now I'm Here/Dreamer's Ball /Love Of My Life/'39/Keep Yourself Alive /Don't Stop Me Now/Spread Your Wings /Brighton Rock/ Mustapha /Bohemian Rhapsody/ Tie Your Mother Down /Sheer Heart Attack/ We Will Rock You/We Are The Champions/ God Save The Queen
EMI EMSP 330 June 1979.

THE GAME
Play The Game/Dragon Attack/Another One Bites The Dust/Need Your Loving Tonight/Crazy Little Thing Called Love/Rock It/Don't Try Suicide/Sail Away Sweet Sister/Coming Soon/Save Me
EMI EMA 795 June 1980.

FLASH GORDON
(ORIGINAL SOUNDTRACK)
Flash's Theme/In The Space Capsule (The Love Theme)/Ming's Theme (In The Court Of Ming The Merciless)/The Ring (Hypnotic Seduction of Dale)/Football Fight/In The Death Cell (Love Theme Reprise)/Execution of Flash/The Kiss (Aura Resurrects Flash)/Arboria (Planet Of The Tree Men)/Escape From The Swamp/Flash To The Rescue/Vultan's Theme (Attack Of The Hawk Men)/Battle Theme/The Wedding March/Marriage of Dale And Ming (And Flash Approaching)/Crash Dive On Mingo Bay/Flash's Theme Reprise (Victory Celebrations)/The Hero
EMI EMC 3351 December 1980.

CONCERT FOR THE PEOPLE OF KAMPUCHEA
(One track only: "Now I'm Here" recorded live at the Hammersmith Odeon benefit concert, 26 December 1979.)
Atlantic K 60153 April 1981.

GREATEST HITS
Bohemian Rhapsody/Another One Bites The Dust/Killer Queen/Fat Bottomed Girls/Bicycle Race/You're My Best Friend/Don't Stop Me Now/Save Me/Crazy Little Thing Called Love/Somebody To Love/Now I'm Here/Good Old Fashioned Lover Boy/Play The Game/Flash/Seven Seas of Rhye/We Will Rock You/We Are The Champions
EMI EMTV 30 October 1981.

HOT SPACE
Staying Power/Dancer/Back Chat/Body Language/Action This Day/Put Out The Fire/Life Is Real (Song for Lennon)/Calling All Girls/Las Palabras De Amour/Cool Cat/Under Pressure
EMI EMA797 May 1982.

THE WORKS
Radio Ga Ga/Tear It Up/It's A Hard Life/Machines (Or Back To Humans)/I Want To Break Free/Keep Passing Open Windows/Hammer To Fall/Is This The World We Created?
EMI EMC 2400141 February 1984.

THE COMPLETE WORKS
A boxed set of Queen's complete recorded output. In addition to the eleven studio albums and the "Live Killers" double album, a new album was included which compiled the singles and "B"-sides otherwise unaccounted for.

COMPLETE VISION
See What A Fool I've Been/A Human Body/Soul Brother/I Go Crazy/Thank God It's Christmas/One Vision/Blurred Vision
EMI QB1 December 1985.

A KIND OF MAGIC
One Vision/A Kind Of Magic/One Year Of Love/Pain Is So Close To Pleasure/Who Wants To Live Forever/Gimme The Prize (Kurgan's Theme)/Don't Lose Your Head/Princes Of The Universe
EMI EU 3509 May 1986.

LIVE MAGIC
One Vision/Tie Your Mother Down/Seven Seas of Rhye/A Kind Of Magic/Under Pressure/Another One Bites The Dust/ I Want To Break Free/Is This The World We Created?/Bohemian Rhapsody/Hammer To Fall/Radio Ga Ga/We Will Rock You/Friends Will Be Friends/We Are The Champions/God Save The Queen
EMI EMC 3519 December 1986.

THE MIRACLE
Party/Khashoggi's Ship/The Miracle/I Want It All/The Invisible Man/Breakthru'/Rain Must Fall/Scandal/My Baby Does Me/Was It All Worth It/Hang On In There (CD only)/ Chinese Torture (CD only)/The Invisible Man (12" version) (CD only)
Parlophone PCSD 107 May 1989.

QUEEN AT THE BEEB
My Fairy King/Keep Yourself Alive/Doing Alright/Liar/Ogre Battle/Great King Rat/Modern Times Rock N'Roll/Son and Daughter
Band of Joy BOYLP/MC/CD 001
December 1989.

INNUENDO
Innuendo/I'm Going Slightly Mad/Headlong/I Can't Live With You/Ride The Wild Wind/All God's People/These Are The Days Of Our Lives/Delilah/Don't Try Too Hard/The Hitman/Bijou/The Show Must Go On
Parlophone PCSD 115 February 1991.

GREATEST HITS II
A Kind Of Magic/Under Pressure/Radio Ga Ga/ I Want It All/I Want To Break Free/ Innuendo/It's A Hard Life/Breakthru/ Who Wants To Live Forever/Headlong/ The Miracle/I'm Going Slightly Mad/ The Invisible Man/Hammer To Fall/ Friends Will Be Friends/The Show Must Go On/ One Vision
Parlophone PCDP7-979712 October 1991.

LIVE AT WEMBLEY
One Vision/Tie Your Mother Down/In The Lap Of The Gods/Seven Seas Of Rhye/ Tear It Up/A Kind Of Magic/Under Pressure/ Another One Bites The Dust/Who Wants To Live Forever/I Want To Break Free/Brighton Rock Solo (May)/Now I'm Here/Love Of My Life/Is This The World We Created/(You're So Square) Baby I Don't Care (Leiber/Stoller)/ Hello Mary Lou (Gene Pitney)/ Tutti Fruitti (Penniman/LaBostrie)/ Gimme Some Lovin' (Winwood/Winwood/Davis)/ Bohemian Rhapsody/Hammer To Fall /Crazy Little Thing Called Love/Big Spender (Coleman/Fields)/Radio Ga-Ga/We Will Rock You/Friends Will Be Friends/ We Are The Champions/God Save The Queen (Trad. arr. May)
Parlophone 7 99594 2 May 1992.

6/96 (24500)